POPPIES
in the
CORN

POPPIES
in the
CORN

FAY GARRISON

ISIS
LARGE PRINT
Oxford

First published in Great Britain 2009
by
History into Print
an imprint of Brewin Books Ltd.

Published in Large Print 2010 by ISIS Publishing Ltd.,
7 Centremead, Osney Mead, Oxford OX2 0ES
by arrangement with
Brewin Book Ltd.

British Library Cataloguing in Publication Data
Garrison, Fay.
    Poppies in the corn. - - (Reminiscence)
    1. Garrison, Fay.
    2. World War, 1939–1945 - - Social aspects - -
    England - - Birmingham.
    3. Country life - - England - - Hampshire - -
    History - - 20th century.
    4. Women teachers - - England - - Biography.
    5. Teachers - - England - - Biography.
    6. Large type books.
    I. Title II. Series
    942.4'96082'092–dc22

        ISBN 978–0–7531–9576–5 (hb)
        ISBN 978–0–7531–9577–2 (pb)

Printed and bound in Great Britain by
T. J. International Ltd., Padstow, Cornwall

Contents

Preface

I remember vividly much of my life as a child living in a rural Hampshire village during World War II. This book is substantially an account of that time viewed from a period several decades later.

I apologise to any reader who may find the occasional inaccuracy among the facts as I recall them. Please bear in mind that the events about which I write are my memories of them when aged between five and eleven years and as such are therefore subject to a child's possible (even likely!) misinterpretation.

Names of people mentioned in the book are correct (as I remember them) with the exception of those I have genuinely forgotten or those I consider might prefer to remain anonymous, for whom in both cases I have introduced fictional names.

I am indebted to Joanna Marshall of Redenham who for the past year has been sending me copies of ARC, the regular monthly newsletter for the local area, and to my sister, Marian, my erstwhile "partner-in-crime" in this idyllic setting for an unforgettable childhood.

Fay Garrison.

CHAPTER ONE

Redenham

During the summer of 1939 in a move to avoid the bombs he was convinced would shortly fall on Birmingham, my father rented for us a rather run-down bungalow in the tiny Hampshire village of Redenham, a few miles from Andover. My mother, a city girl all her life, was horrified. Anything rural was anathema to her, from the dark country roads to the watchful cows in the fields. The fact that the bungalow was at the end of a much pot-holed lane in the middle of an orchard at least half a mile from the nearest neighbour was enough to cause her sleepless nights and resorts to the sherry bottle.

By the end of May 1940 Dad would be despatched to France with the British Expeditionary Force where he would become swallowed up in the military machinations of the defence of Calais and ultimate exodus from Dunkirk. Unfortunately for him, his duty as a member of the Rifle Brigade meant that he would be one of the rear-guard action team who was not permitted to escape in the famous flotilla of small boats to be sent from the mainland to bring home those exposed on the Dunkirk beaches. Along with several thousand others, he would be captured and frog-marched over a hundred miles into Germany where he'd be held prisoner in Stalag 383 until the end of the war.

The safety of the family had been his main concern and the concept of the forthcoming war infringing itself on the rural idyll of this quiet little hamlet was unthinkable. Nevertheless, children went to school daily armed with gas-masks and the local bobby frequently took his life in his hands to venture up our hazardous lane in the darkness on his bicycle to warn our mother that cracks of light were showing in the blackout.

Redenham was an idyllic setting for my sister, Marian, and for me, even if it was not our mother's ideal choice of habitat. My abiding memory of the place is of eternal sunshine and blue skies with poppy-splashed fields of waving golden corn and countless hidden dens beneath the hazel, sloe and hawthorn bushes. Children at that time were free to roam at will and often spent hours at play out of doors without the supervision of adults.

No one appeared to be wary of allowing us this freedom. Even if we did have the occasional potentially dangerous experience we tended not to inform our elders of the fact! I remember falling from the top of a haystack onto the metal blade of a plough and although I suffered considerable pain and bruising, did not tell Mum about it and shrugged off her questions regarding the evidence. Likewise meeting up with the odd character whose apparent interest in children and consequent suspicious behaviour, was something we'd most likely leave our friend Arthur, slightly older than us, to deal with rather than tell our mother! I am sure it would have been different if our childhood had been spent in The Midlands.

Much as I love my home town of Birmingham it is the memory of Redenham that has stayed with me throughout my life. I still dream regularly of the place almost seventy years on. Marian and I have been back to visit several times and have been delighted to find it little changed since the time we were there. The bungalow eventually became a store-shed for a local farmer's tractor and the beautiful orchard was cut down, but there's enough left for us to reminisce and recall our childhood pastimes.

Stationed at Tidworth, just across the county border in Wiltshire, meant that Dad was able to come home on his motor-bike from time to time before war was officially declared. I loved to sit on his knee and bury my face in his rough uniform. It may have been for that reason that following his last visit I contracted meningitis, which I understand during the epidemic of the disease at the time tended to be rife in such close communities as army barracks, even though my father himself never suffered from it and mine was the only case in our neighbourhood.

I can still remember the fierce headache at the start of my illness and being violently sick over the vicar's shoes (he wore gaiters) outside our village post office. This was shortly before my fifth birthday.

There followed a strangely unforgettable period of several weeks in Tidworth military hospital which I remember in a white mist: nurses' uniforms, mother's face behind a mask (her visits were few because it was deemed unsettling for children to see parents too frequently!), friendships with other sick children, many of whom were to die during my stay, and the gathering of heavy-hanging clouds, that I was terrified were about to fall on me, outside the window behind my bed. The latter was not a subject I ever spoke of because I knew it sounded ridiculous, but when much later I was to read at school the story of Chicken Licken, who thought the sky was falling after an acorn dropped onto his head, I felt I'd found a kindred spirit. Even now those clouds have a habit of re-appearing in my dreams whenever I feel stressed.

Just two or three years too soon to benefit from the first uses of penicillin, I suppose I was lucky to be one who survived the disease. For good reasons of her own, my mother decided I needed to convalesce with her brother and his wife back in Birmingham, to where I was despatched on leaving hospital.

CHILDHOOD MEMORY
I remember
looking up beneath an arch of roses,
the air alive with insect wings;
beyond, the sky a speedwell blue
and hung about with still white clouds,

But my heart was heavy.
Far away from here
my daddy was at war
and I had just become aware
that it was possible
he may never stand again
beneath this arch with me.

Fay Garrison,
written for Earlsdon Writers, 1995.

CHAPTER
TWO

The Aviary

Uncle Joe and Aunt Gertrude had no children of their own and considerably more money than we had, so could afford the small luxuries Mum had been told were necessary to restore the flesh to my bones and roses to my cheeks.

Theirs was a terraced house, very neat and tidy, with delicate china figurines crowded onto every available surface. And silence. There were times when the rooms seemed so devoid of sound that I would stand before the wall clock in the parlour and watch the slow-swinging pendulum through the glass door just to hear its reassuring tick.

Aunt Gertrude was several years older than her husband and had the appearance and demeanour of one who had never been young. Though scarcely beyond her early forties, she shuffled along like an ailing eighty-year-old. Her thin shoulders were covered summer and winter alike with a thick shawl and she spent her days polishing or washing her many ornaments. Her evenings were spent silently watching the flames dance in the grate.

But she loved me. I don't remember her ever sitting me on her knee or hugging me the way my mother did, yet, in spite of her severe manner, I felt secure in the knowledge that I was wanted here. I missed the company of my little sister, Mum's cooking and the comfortable lack of regime in my own home, but I grew accustomed to the new strict household routine.

Uncle Joe, on the other hand, was a joy. To me, now that war had begun and Dad's brief visits home had come to an end, he was a surrogate father. Uncle Joe had already done his bit for his country in World War I, where he'd been gassed in the trenches of Ypres, — or "Wipers," as he called it — and now worked at the Birmingham Small Arms factory just down the road.

I loved Uncle Joe's Popeye-like toothy grin (he possessed one visible tooth of his own and wore his dentures only on Sundays). I loved the smell of him in his factory overalls when he swung me into his arms on his arrival home each day. I loved the long walks we had together when he would tell me tales of the escapades he and my mother had got up to in their childhood. And most of all I loved his aviary.

The aviary was Uncle Joe's pride and joy. It took up the whole width and the bottom six feet of the narrow back garden, two thirds of it consisting of wooden-framed narrow-gauge wire netting. The rest was a shed that doubled as nesting areas for the birds and storage for the garden tools.

There were two varieties of birds: canaries and budgerigars. From as far away as the living room window I never tired of watching the vivid streaks of brilliant blues, greens and yellows as they darted from perch to perch in their lovingly-constructed habitat. At weekends I was allowed to help sweep out and wash the perches.

On one magical day, I was beckoned silently into the shed and given a tiny warm white egg to hold in its nesting box. When it was hatched a few weeks later I had the privilege of naming the new arrival. I called it Topsy after my favourite doll.

Summer came and went very slowly. I understood that it would be spring again before I would be returned to my own family. I would have been away from them for about fifteen months. In spite of occasional visits from my mother and sister I was desperately homesick.

During one such visit I tried to persuade two-year-old Marian to come and see my beloved Topsy in the aviary. Halfway down the garden she began to cry and ran back to hide her face in Mum's skirt. I longed to do the same thing but was conscious that it was the kind of behaviour that would not please Aunt Gertrude. The discovery that I had apparently become a stranger to my little sister was quite a shock.

In November the bombing began. I had started school by then and was, even after several weeks, having difficulties with the new regime. Utter confusion over playtime and lunch breaks meant I was constantly walking home at the wrong time and being pursued by teachers from one direction or escorted by my aunt from another.

Gas mask drill took up each Friday afternoon and the brick air-raid shelters in the playground were barely erected before the first day-time siren was sounded. At home, Uncle Joe had built an Anderson shelter in front of the aviary.

"Shall we take the birds in there with us?" I asked him, not feeling inclined to leave them to the mercy of the bombs.

"No, they wouldn't like to be shut up in the dark," Uncle Joe assured me.

Their welfare was my first concern on emerging from the shelter each morning.

It was cold in the shelter but there was an element of adventure and excitement about it all. The theatrical effect created by the massive searchlights sweeping across a midnight sky as I was zipped into my siren suit and rushed into the shelter, to the accompaniment of the air-raid warning signal, appealed to my sense of drama.

As the bombing became a regular occurrence during the rest of that month, it was soon our habit to take to the shelter nightly soon after dusk.

One morning, on scrambling out into the daylight, the air felt surprisingly warm. As I glanced towards the aviary, my heart missed a beat. For one dreaded moment I thought it had gone.

Gradually, stumbling and coughing through a heavy smoke-laden fog, I began dimly to trace the outline of the cages with a sense of relief.

Standing before them was my Uncle Joe. In his warden's duty helmet and overalls from the night's

9

activities, he appeared to be standing to attention like a soldier. And the birds were singing.

Tentatively I touched my uncle's hand. He looked down at me and smiled, his face stained with smoke and grime, as two white streaks ran down from his eyes. It frightened me to realise they had been made by tears.

"Sing, my beauties," he said, looking at the birds. "Sing loud. You have a lot of singing to do today."

"Why, Uncle?" I asked.

"You see, Fay, a lot of people were killed last night in the bombing," he explained. "And their souls have to go on a long, long journey up to Heaven. They travel that much faster on the wings of birdsong. I think our birds know that."

Aunt Gertrude was packing a suitcase when we went into the house for breakfast.

"Uncle can't go to work today because the factory's been bombed," she told me. {We're going to your mother's in Redenham, Fay, for Christmas."

Sitting on the train with Topsy in a cage on the seat beside me, I couldn't help singing too.

"I wonder why the birds sang today," Aunt Gertrude said. "I suppose they thought spring had come in the warmth from the fires last night."

I looked at Uncle Joe and he winked. We knew different, I thought, and grinned back at him . . .

CHAPTER
THREE

Appleshaw School

Although Aunt Gertrude and Uncle Joe stayed on at our country retreat for a couple of months, it gradually became clear that it was not expected that I should go back to Birmingham with them when the time came. Either my mother had a change of heart because of the bombing or other members of her family persuaded her it was not in my best interests, particularly, as I discovered later, Aunt Gertrude was intent on adopting me. This did not happen. So after the Christmas holiday, since there was no school in Redenham itself, I started attending the one in Appleshaw, the neighbouring village.

Now aged five I was tested for my first reading book. When it was discovered that I could read all the early infant readers, thanks to the teaching of Nancy, Aunt Gertrude's ten-year-old neighbour, (the girl achieved this miracle with the aid of "The Baby's Jolly Book" and raps across the knuckles with a ruler!), I was given a series of Hans Andersen Fairy Tales, which led to an affection that remains to this day. I sometimes wonder if Nancy as an adult may have become a teacher.

On account of my reading ability I was promoted to "First Class" which was located across the aisle from "The Babies" since in our two-teacher school both classes were in the same room. It was apparently expected that my writing and number skills would equal that of the reading. But they didn't. This sphere of my education obviously hadn't ranked particularly highly in Nancy's estimation. I was given a book ruled with lines and told to copy a sentence from the blackboard. No amount of lip-biting, tongue-extending or finger-gripping could persuade my pencil to get my unwieldy letters to sit on those lines. Likewise when I was faced with two digits, one above the other with two parallel lines beneath them and told to "add the numbers," I was mystified.

My favourite subject was history. The headteacher, Miss Williams-Freeman, who taught Standards 2 to 4 in the other classroom, would change places with our infants teacher, Miss Loader, once a week to take us for this lesson. I was enraptured by her stories of Sharptooth, the little Stoneage boy, who went hunting with a flint-tipped spear and had his first taste of cooked meat following a forest fire.

The teacher for the infants class was Miss Loader. Amazingly, it was her own specialist subject that eventually grew to become my ultimate lifetime passion: music. I say "amazingly" because the lady was one of the most uncharismatic teachers I was ever to encounter. She wore a permanent inscrutably grim expression on her face and dealt harshly with the infants, even the new little five-year-olds. Much of her teaching was done with the aid of a "pointer" which she used to demonstrate facts from the blackboard, denote our position on the times tables chart (chanted daily) and to rap the knuckles of the nail-biters, of which I was one. We were terrified of her and all our schoolwork was conducted in total silence.

I don't remember any music lessons at all during the time I was in her class, which was about two years, but when I was moved into Standard 2 in the other classroom there was an hour or so a week when the two teachers exchanged classes so that Miss Loader could give the older pupils a music lesson with the added use of a piano.

These were magical. I was introduced for the first time to songs from The National Song Book, of which we were all given copies of the words, as well as hymns and Christmas carols in season. I remember learning the tune to The First Nowell and thinking it the most beautiful song ever written. I spent hours on visits to my grandmother in Birmingham picking out the notes for it on the piano in her freezing cold front parlour. Over those three years we sang songs by Handel, Schubert, Bach, Arne and others and were even taught to sing the occasional two-part chorus as well as countless rounds. My sister and I can still perform a two-part setting of "You spotted snakes with double tongue" learnt when we were eight and ten years old!

Lessons always started with solfa-reading from a "Modulator" that was fixed to the blackboard. It remains in my head to this day when I am faced with a new piece of music to sing, even though long ago I learned to read notes written on a stave.

There was a memorable incident that had the effect of permanently revising our image of Miss Loader though I am not sure that she saw this fact at all favourably.

To walk to Appleshaw School, some children had to cross fields from Ragged Appleshaw on the other side of the village. There was a bull in one of the fields nearest the school, usually tethered. It was said later that some boys had earlier taunted the bull with sticks and unknown to anyone at the time, had managed to pull loose its tethering. As the children, around a dozen or so, crossed the field, the bull suddenly came towards them at a gallop, head down and snorting. It happened that Miss Loader also came to school that same way and saw the danger. She called out to the children to run towards the style at the bottom of the hill near to the school, which they did, while she remained stationary facing the charging animal. She was gored and butted and spent some time in hospital following the incident.

Although Miss Loader's teaching style continued to be conducted as it always had been, somehow the children's attitude towards her changed. We were no longer a class of grudgingly attentive pupils with a pitiless martinet as our teacher. We had all learned to love Jesus who gave his life for us on the cross and now we began to learn to like — if not quite to love — our brave teacher who had done likewise in facing and being wounded by a savage bull for our sakes. We thanked her silently in our hearts just as we thanked Jesus silently in our prayers.

There was at the time no provision made for pupils at school during lunchtimes. No teacher remained on the premises and there were no meals on offer. Practically all the children went home for lunch. A handful of us whose mothers were at work took sandwiches (jam sandwiches in the case of my sister and me) and ate them under the trees on the green that surrounded the playground, completely unsupervised. My sister's friend Jean, whose mother was a teacher, had a grandmother living in the row of cottages nearby and Marian and I frequently accompanied Jean there after our lunch and were treated to a cup of Ovaltine.

Jean's Grandad occasionally joined us on his lunch-break from the local forge where he was the blacksmith. We were sometimes allowed to watch him at work from the forge doorway. It was the most impressive sight: Mr Blake, sweating profusely, his shirt-sleeves rolled up above his elbows, swinging his hammer to shape a red-hot horse-shoe beside the blazing furnace. There was always work for him since there were several big country houses in the district with stables, including one owned by a branch of the Guinness family.

I was to spend the best part of my primary school days at Appleshaw School and passed the eleven-plus examination on reaching Standard 4.

On our family's return to Birmingham and my transition for the summer term of that year to a large primary school, I was completely and utterly confused by the different atmosphere, teaching methods, children's attitudes both to me and to each other and the sheer number of pupils all around me in the classroom and playground. My performance in the end-of-year tests resulted in humiliatingly low marks, which made my mother thank our lucky stars I'd already got the eleven-plus "in the bag". I'm convinced I'd never have passed this examination had I had to endure more time in what I considered to be such an adverse environment.

It stood me well, my time at Appleshaw School, and I think the quality of the teaching I received to be among the best of its kind. Marian, likewise, passed her eleven-plus two years later, having benefited equally from the years she spent there.

CHAPTER
FOUR

Facts of Life

Innocence is a word that has long been associated with children and the young. Whether we interpret this in connection with thoughts or deeds is not necessarily apparent. It tends to be linked with the awareness of sex. We appear to regard the inexperience of children in this field, along with their assumed lack of knowledge on the subject, as evidence of purity of mind.

At the time I was a child at Appleshaw school, prior to the use of artificial insemination in animal husbandry, a good proportion of children in the village would have, from an early age, witnessed taking the cows to the bull for the purposes of mating as well as painting the ram's thighs with dye in order to be sure that the ewes were covered for the same reason.

Does this mean that country children were therefore lacking in innocence or somehow impure? I would not have thought so. It did not demand a high IQ to apply what they had seen to the behaviour of males and females in general. And having learned these interesting facts at first hand, would it not be quite natural to want to share what they knew with others not so well informed? Being one of the latter, I was soon to be given a frank lesson on the subject at the tender age of seven going on eight.

I was now in Standard 1, still under the rigorous authority of Miss Loader, in a row of double-seated "proper" desks at the back of the classroom. My desk partner was Billy Mills, a tough, clever boy with a fair comprehension of life and a limitless vocabulary of swear words. We shared the honour of being the best readers in the class.

He was also very good at maths. Nor did he mind my copying his answers, which enabled me for the first time to merit a few ticks among the endless crosses in my sum book.

His reward was for me to allow him occasionally to put his arm around my waist. This progressed to a hand on my knee. However, when his hand started to slide up my leg towards my knicker elastic, I decided this was enough! I glared at him and met with a bemused smirk as he clutched harder at my leg. It was only when I raised my arm as if to attract the teacher's attention that he withdrew his hand. This did not deter him completely, but the slightest threat "to tell" was enough to prevent any further experiments on his part.

But Billy hadn't quite finished his obvious desire to educate me on a subject high on his agenda. He took me aside in the playground one day and sat me down on the cinder floor beside the rain-water butt so that we were away from the other children.

"Yer know what girls and boys is supposed to do?" he said, in his broad southern counties brogue.

"What?" I said.

"Yer know boys' cocks and girls' cocks is different?"

"Course I do," I answered. I was not lacking in this knowledge, having seen my friend Arthur put out small fires a few times using this part of his anatomy.

"Girls is made so's boys can put their'n inside 'em," said Billy.

"They're never," I said.

Had not playtime been cut short by the school bell, I daresay a practical demonstration might well have been on the cards!

I may not have understood exactly what Billy meant at first but found myself thinking it over later and gradually filling in the gaps of what little information I'd acquired before and making some sense of it all.

Somehow friends of mine seemed to realise that I was now one of those qualified to listen to the risqué jokes that were apparently a routine topic of conversation among my classmates. I did not necessarily understand them all but one or two became clearer following my initiation by Billy Mills regarding the basic facts of life as he had described them to me.

Nevertheless, when Marian and I saw our white cock jumping on the hens at home, we continued to clobber it with a broom. Two and two did not add up to four in this situation. But then, my grasp of maths never was very good!

CHAPTER
FIVE

Neighbours

We lived two hundred or so yards from the main village of Redenham and almost the same distance from our nearest neighbours who had a bungalow in the centre of the orchard. This was the home of Eunice and Bob Eyles, who were to become lifelong friends of my parents. They had come from Jersey in the Channel Islands. Whether they had fled Jersey because of the occupation of the Channel Islands by the Nazis I never discovered, though I suspect they were living in Redenham some time before that happened. After the war they returned to Jersey and became farmers, eventually setting up what became a flourishing business growing tomatoes. I remember at least one very happy holiday there, my parents visiting them on several further occasions later.

Their son, Arthur, a year older than me, was my closest friend during my time in Redenham. He was both my boy-friend and my protector. He called for me each day going to school and although he always persuaded me to go ahead of him before reaching the end of our lane, he continued to look out for me when reaching the main road and his friends, the three

Futcher boys and Billy Mills, caught up with us. Innocent that I was, I feared no danger from boys of any age, but Arthur knew his friends and I fancy he had his suspicions regarding the possible taunting and more serious profanities to which I might have been exposed had he not been looking out for me.

Arthur was my champion and my hero: tall, plump, freckle-faced and gentle. With his mates he was tough and coarsely-spoken with a broad local accent and the usual unsavoury vocabulary. On our own he was kind, affectionate and demonstrative, as he was also with his baby sister, Dawn.

He kept ferrets; nasty snappy little creatures that he used to catch rabbits. He was a typical country boy with an ingenuity for finding birds' eggs, frequently putting his hand at random into a bush and taking them out as if he knew by instinct where they were. The eggs were then "blown" and added to his collection or occasionally given as a gift to me. Our headmistress would occasionally ask who had taken birds' eggs and most of the offenders (always boys) were surprisingly honest and lined up to receive the official punishment: one stroke of the cane on the palm of the hand. It was the only sin that merited the cane. I have since wondered if the boys' reasons for confessing their actions were perhaps a rather macho pride at being able to withstand this obviously painful admonishment.

In the autumn we, together with the Eyles family, picked apples in the orchard. This was paid work, even for children, at so much a basket. Gypsies provided the larger part of the workforce, mainly those who lived locally for most of the year in traditional caravans in nearby Chute. The gypsy children did not attend school although all the youngsters became very friendly and we often visited each other. I loved their caravans and envied their attractive lifestyle, sitting around bonfires in the evenings, cooking and eating meals out of doors.

The gypsies also helped with the potato harvest. This always seemed to happen during term-time, but apparently merited legitimate time off school. It was back-breaking work but well-paid (at least it was so for us children). I remember looking at my shiny two-shilling piece very proudly — I don't recall whether this was for a day's work or a week's!

Redenham had its own resident gypsy who lived in a railway carriage at the roadside. How on earth it came to be there has remained a mystery to me all my life. The interesting fact is that I saw it was still there recently, over fifty years later, having been given a new roof and surrounded by a well-tended garden! The resident during the forties was the grandmother of a friend of mine, Thomasina Wardle, whose father was a professional photographer in Appleshaw. I was once invited with Thomasina to tea at her Granny's unconventional home and was quite taken aback at the comparative luxury of the décor inside the unprepossessing exterior of the building.

The old lady was the epitome of the traditional gypsy, with iron-grey hair plaited and coiled around her gold-ringed ears, a face like wrinkled brown leather and a tendency to predict the fortunes of whomsoever she engaged in conversation. On the occasion our mother had received news from the Ministry of War that our Dad was missing, presumed killed, she met up with us on our way to Appleshaw post office to collect Mum's widow's pension for the first time. The old lady, before a word had been spoken, put her hand on Mum's arm and said,

"Dinna grieve, Mrs Wadderzit," (a name she called everyone). "He be alive and well, you'll see."

And her words came true. Mum received the news a few weeks later that Dad was a prisoner of war.

There was what my mother called a "Borstal" in Chute. We'd probably call it a Probationers' Hostel nowadays. The residents had leave to go into the village at weekends. Mum was quite paranoid about these young men (there appeared to be no women there) who were in the habit of knocking on our door frequently for water, ours being the first house en route to the village of Appleshaw. She tended to open the door clutching Dad's (illegal!) poacher's gun, which was shaped like a walking stick, presumably to deter any "funny business"!!

At the end of our lane on the main road to Appleshaw lived the Futcher family. My sister Marian, before starting school, was often in the care of Mrs Futcher while Mum was at work at the ROAC in Chute, to which she travelled on her bicycle. The three Futcher boys were Arthur's best friends and therefore often involved with my sister and me in the making of bonfires and roasting "pignuts" that we dug up from under the beech trees. We two girls were very much "onlookers" rather than partakers in these boys' activities, though tolerated because Arthur was our friend.

Our other neighbour was our landlord, Mr Pound. He lived in the big house on the other side of the orchard. He was the archetypal country squire in his plus-fours, gaiters, panama hat, with a gun permanently under his arm whenever we met him. He owned most of the land and business in Redenham.

Our mother was quite overwhelmed at the welcome we received from him and from his wife on our arrival in Redenham, almost as if we were members of his own family. I imagine that this may have been due to respect for the fact that Dad, even as a lowly Lance Corporal, was on active service in the war when few others in the neighbourhood were likewise involved.

Mr Pound's son, Neil, who ran much of his father's business and owned several lorries for the purpose of transporting fruit and vegetables grown locally, lived in a large newly-built house in Redenham. He was a very handsome young man with an equally beautiful wife and there was much talk among the sensation-seeking pupils of Appleshaw School of "irregular goings-on" at their big house in the way of roisterous wine-drinking parties at which women danced naked on tables! Although some of the pupils may have had parents who worked at the house, I imagine many of these tales were invented by the children themselves! It certainly did not sit well with our picture of the older members of the family. I remember Neil Pound's two small children starting school and as a junior pupil hearing them say their letters in the babies' class. They were not at our school for very long, presumably because they would have eventually attended a private one.

We were frequently invited by Mrs Pound (senior) to their home for afternoon tea (very formal, with delicate china teacups) and Marian and I were given free access to their family library, being allowed to borrow the whole collection of the Arthur Mee children's encyclopaedias during a time when books were not easily accessible.

The most enjoyable times for me were the musical afternoons held in the Pounds' magnificent formal drawing room, with gilt-framed family portraits on the walls and an imposing concert grand piano. Mother would take along her music and Mrs Pound would accompany her in the popular songs of the day: Somewhere a Voice is Calling, Bless this House, Trees, When all was Young and Pleasant May was Blooming, The Jewels of the Madonna from Faust, Handel's Largo and many more.

Mrs Pound was a genteel lady with a lovely speaking voice (I often tried to imitate her in order to acquire a similar accent), and she always wore a small straw hat indoors, rather like those Queen Elizabeth (wife of King George VI) wore, but with a narrower brim. And she was a superb pianist.

Occasionally when I was not well, Mrs Pound would look after me while Mum was at work, although I was made to lie on the chaise-longue in her sitting room and to drink green liquid peppermint which I hated!

This introduction to a completely different way of life from anything I'd ever known before, in a pre-television era, was an education in itself.

It was Mr Pound who was to fetch Dad from Andover Station when he was released from the prison camp several weeks after the war was over. We waited with Mum under the rose-arch in our new clothes made especially for the occasion, as Pound's van chugged up the lane to the bungalow. The moment Dad stepped out of the van is written indelibly on my brain as if a finger has been pressed on the pause button of a video film. I am aware of the three of us under the sweet-scented rose-arch and the sight of our Dad, thin and pale in his army uniform, a few seconds before he gathered us into his arms. Mr Pound must have made a lightening exit because I remember nothing of him or his van after that moment, though his role in Dad's homecoming had been crucial.

As a young teenager I often used to make a list of those who I regarded were closest to my heart. The Pounds and Arthur were among these and probably remain there to this day, several decades later.

CHAPTER
SIX

Lime Green

It is a common shade in our post-war era. We are confronted with it everywhere to attract our attention, the iridescent neon version in particular.

But to me the shade lime-green is linked irrevocably with parachutes. In fact, as I recall it, much of my childhood seems to have been enacted before a backdrop of hazy greenish-yellow.

It was inevitable that the extensive canopy of open fields in the area where we lived would eventually be discovered by the RAF, who found the district around Redenham and Appleshaw an ideal training ground for its young pilots. One day the cows in the field on the opposite side of our lane were gone and the air was filled with the constant roar of aeroplanes taking off. Our isolated bungalow became overnight the Mecca of the village for our mother's work colleagues from the RAOC who were eager to become acquainted with the sudden influx of beautiful young men who seemed constantly to be knocking on our door asking for water or matches.

When the RAF in due course set up camp in a hitherto little-used farm building, the villagers found they had access to the luxury of a local cinema, albeit small-scale with a somewhat noisy projector. Acquaintance with one of the servicemen being the only qualification for admission made the new residents even more popular with the locals.

It was on the way back from one of these rare trips, having seen a memorable production of "Scrooge", that we discovered the parachute. All three of us, my mother, sister and I, literally "walked into it" where it lay, stretched across the whole width of the lane in front of our bungalow. Even in the darkness its colour became gradually quite identifiable as an almost fluorescent lime-green.

Marian and I were quite convinced it had transported a German spy into our midst and the two of us spent the following days scouring disused pig-sties and barns for sight of him. Exactly what we'd have done if we had discovered our spy is unclear, although the excitement lasted for several days.

For reasons of her own, our mother forbade us to talk of our "find" to friends at school. Her desire for secrecy we interpreted as confirmation of our suspicions that it was connected with the enemy and we had been well-schooled via bill-boards and the wireless that "careless talk costs lives."

The only person to be trusted with the information was our mother's friend, Dot. Like us, Dot was something of a "foreigner" in the village, having come from Lancashire with her soldier husband, who before being sent to France, had been stationed a few miles away. I suspect our two families were tolerated, in spite of what must have appeared our rather odd accents, because our fathers were the only men from the village representing Redenham's part in the war, most of the other males having "reserved occupation" status for their work on the land.

It was Dot's idea that the parachute should be "treated" by being submerged inside a large rainwater butt. This served a double purpose: it was possible to keep it contained and therefore hidden (under a tarpaulin) and having been given a good soaking for a couple of days the rather stiff fabric became more pliable. When it was opened out to dry, its size was vast, extending to every corner of the garden. Our mother and her friend then set about cutting it into manageable-sized squares that were hastily taken indoors before anyone should observe what was going on.

For the next few weeks and months — indeed it felt like years, at least for the remainder of the war — our mother was rarely to be seen without a lap piled high with the gaudy fabric, labouring over the current garment in production. It was a similar scene at our Aunt Dot's house. Whilst all the other children in the village continued to wear their much-worn, let-down and patched "sensible" clothes, Dot's children and the two of us were suddenly conspicuous in our brilliant skirts, dresses and trousers. I remember a particular "bolero" (ie a short-sleeved jacket without fastenings) which I wore for a few years. Although attempts were made to ensure that my sister and I also had countless pairs of knickers in the same material, these were hastily discarded due to the irritation the fabric created on certain sensitive areas of our anatomy.

There was never any positive conclusion to this particular episode in my childhood. Whether or not the parachute had been the property of the British or that of our enemy we were never to discover. But in the stringent shortages of the day, a dearth of clothing coupons not the least of them, our rare find had proved invaluable.

CHAPTER
SEVEN

The Americans

Our quiet rural retreat changed overnight the moment America joined us in the war. A contingent of the army was based at Ludgershall, across the county border in Wiltshire, about two miles from Redenham. The whole neighbourhood welcomed them readily, including the pupils of Appleshaw School.

On the first of their many marches through our village, the children ran down to the roadside at the edge of the school field to welcome them. They rewarded us by throwing us sweets, gum and money. Our pockets were bulging with these rich pickings when one of the teachers rang the bell for the end of playtime.

Our resentment at having to put all the money into the Waifs and Strays charity box was considerable. But at least we were allowed to keep the sweets and gum, which were rare treats since these were strictly rationed. On similar future occasions we learned to cheat and hide money in our knicker-legs — at least the girls did. Presumably the boys found other means of concealing their plunder, having been forced to turn out their pockets.

Local nightlife blossomed with the presence of the American forces in the area. The village hall had not previously encountered such thriving activity. There were suddenly dances, whist-drives, parties and even with the privations of clothing coupons, a one-off fashion show. With the arrival of a family of evacuees in our home (all three of us having to crowd into one bedroom to accommodate them), and therefore resident baby-sitters, Mum found herself suddenly able to take advantage of this new social life, encouraged by Aunt Dot.

Dot loved the American soldiers. She had no reservations about dating several of them, giving her something of a reputation among the local housewives (who, of course, had husbands at home to keep an eye on them, limiting their own activities somewhat). As far as our mother was concerned, there was just one GI who became quite a regular visitor to our bungalow. He was Lieutenant Pinkerton. I do believe Mum only befriended him because of his name. She was a very keen singer and had had professional voice coaching from a Madame Lillian Green in Birmingham in her youth. (The best part of her wages from the Lucas's factory where she worked until she was married had been spent on these lessons). We knew it had been her ambition to become an opera singer, so when Pinkie came on the scene I think she was wooed by his name as much as anything else, Lieutenant Pinkerton being the tenor in Puccini's *Madame Butterfly*.

I still have no idea how far our mother's relationship went with her Pinkie, although I would be surprised if it was ever a sexual one, judging from her attitude towards this subject and what I understood later to be her reluctance to indulge in it! I remember him as a very kind, generous man, who seemed to enjoy the company of our family, mother and daughters alike. He gave me a silver dollar when he left.

This was to cause me a severe grilling by my dad after he came home when he found me turning out my moneybox one day. I admitted to him that I'd received it from "Pinkie". Did Pinkie ever stay the night, he wanted to know. How often did he come to the house? Did I ever see him kissing Mum? My replies were guarded and if anything erred on the side of being deliberately negative. I was aged ten by that time and knew a thing or two about relationships, particularly after the Americans had been living nearby. The fact that Dad's close friend, Derek, who'd been in the Rifle Brigade with him, came home to find he had a beautiful blond, blue-eyed son of three after his five-year stint in the war, was enough to make Dad suspicious of the Americans on our doorstep. There was an ironic outcome to the story of Derek and his family. Having accepted his wife's love-child (who grew to be a lovely young man) the couple had a child of their own. This was a girl with impaired growth, whom we labelled at the time a dwarf. Our families remained friends for many years after the war.

There were a number of liaisons with the GIs by girls in the villages of Appleshaw and Redenham during the brief time they were stationed locally. I know of at least one resulting in an illegitimate baby and consequently a source of much sniggering and lewd story-telling by the pupils of Appleshaw School. There were others who became GI brides and went off to America with their new partners. Aunty Dot mourned the going of the Americans more than most. Her own marriage survived less than twelve months after her husband came home.

The Americans were not long in Ludgershall, which I assume had been a training camp before they were sent to fight in the war in France. With their going and the RAF pilots now fully-trained and probably stationed nearer the coastal regions, our rural community reverted to its original uneventful status.

As far as the pupils of Appleshaw School were concerned, we found ourselves short on salacious subjects about which to make jokes. We had to satisfy our unwholesome appetites for such matters with the antics of the local pervert, who removed the pin from Joy Brown's knickers in the woods after Sunday School.

CHAPTER
EIGHT

Pigs and Poultry

Rationing for country dwellers was not such an ordeal as it must have been for those in the towns. Admittedly we had limited access to such luxuries as sweets and sugar, but there was always a way round many of the other shortages. Milk, honey, fruit and vegetables were always available and someone somewhere was bound to be killing a pig at reasonable intervals. Most people kept hens in their back gardens, so eggs and the occasional stewed or roast chicken were frequently on our menus.

A city girl, having been brought up in a family of seven children and a soldier father who'd been disabled in the Boer War with an inadequate army pension, our mother found this sudden access to cheap, and in some cases free food a welcome luxury. It appeared to her to be the one saving grace of being stuck out here in the middle of nowhere. Her abiding memory of her own childhood was one of feeling permanently hungry.

Mum was a good cook and living in an orchard meant there was always an apple pie in the food-safe (a small cupboard with a wire-mesh door to keep out flies). We had wild strawberries and gooseberries growing locally in season as well as hazel, beech and walnuts. Not that I personally ever ate anything but unripe apples straight from the trees. Consequently I was very thin, prone to colds and suffered frequently from stomach-ache!

Our landlord, Mr Pound, owned most of the land in Redenham and apart from a small rose garden at the front of the house there was a vast area of uncultivated wilderness beyond it. Our evacuee family managed to tame quite a lot of it, planting beans, tomatoes and other vegetables, while Mum decided we were going to keep hens.

We set off on the weekly bus to Andover on market day and came back — on the bus! — with two broody hens with their legs tied together in a sack. These were Anne and Betty. Initially, until Mum had managed to "borrow" some sort of pen for them from a local farmer, they were to live in "the conservatory", a rather grand name for the leaky glass-roofed lean-to which ran along the front of the bungalow. We put straw in the two compartments of an orange box, with fertile hen's eggs in one of them and duck-eggs (again from the market) in the other. Anne and Betty duly did their stuff and by the time the eggs were hatched there was a coop for them in the orchard.

Anne "mothered" eight ducklings and Betty eight chicks. The chicks were all given names but we couldn't identify individual ducklings because they were all the same colour. Marian and I dug a hole in the ground, lowered a rusty tin bath into it, which we filled with water, and the ducklings needed no persuasion to jump in. I think this caused their mother, Anne, some permanent psychological damage; she flapped and clucked hysterically for the rest of the day, running round and round the bath-tub, but she never abandoned her babies. We probably exacerbated her mental condition when she became broody a second time by putting three turkey eggs and a goose egg in her nest!

And so began what became quite a respectable poultry farm. We ended up with three geese, three turkeys, eight ducks (though the ducks in their adulthood all died from some disease which didn't seem to affect the other birds) and around thirty or more chickens. We never learned the art of keeping the birds within their coops (although we acquired about three of these) and were constantly chasing chickens and geese out of the house and off the furniture. Mum regularly managed to sell some of the eggs and the occasional unwanted cock while my sister and I persistently refused to eat chicken of any kind. How could we, when we knew all the birds by name? Surprisingly we were not so fussy about the geese or the turkeys, though my personal diet continued to be restricted to sour apples and the odd boiled egg.

Compared with today it is hard to imagine what an onerous business shopping for basic provisions must have been without cars, fridges or even telephones, particularly for working mothers miles from the nearest shops. Mum took us on Saturdays to Ludgershall, more than two miles away (there was no bus so we had to walk) to collect our rations for the week. During one winter, while Marian was still quite small, the grocer must have taken pity on us and although petrol was rationed, started to deliver our groceries fortnightly, leaving them in a cardboard box on the back doorstep just inside the wash-house.

There was no door on our wash-house, a fact discovered within a few weeks of the first delivery by pigs from a local farm who were at the time being given free reign of the orchard to clear up the windfalls. Our mother, having been at work, didn't see the damage until she met up with me arriving home from school. Nothing at all could be salvaged — not even, amazingly enough, the few rashers that constituted our bacon ration!

The farmer was acutely apologetic and gave us a new-born piglet as recompense. The fragile, diminutive, pink creature lasted two days in our loving care, being fed with milk from a baby's bottle and kept warm overnight with a hot-water-bottle under the grate in a straw-filled box. Mum told us it was obviously the "runt" of the litter, a word I have since always associated with small, treasured, beautiful things.

Bonfire night, on November the fifth during wartime, had become a non-event. Bonfires were banned after dark due to the general blackout. However, in the middle of our orchard, it was not difficult to mask illegal activity amid the trees, unless it was seen from the air. I remember one such night, when a bonfire surpassing all bonfires was held in "the pit": a deep sunken cavity in the orchard which had all the appearance of possibly having been made by a meteorite, though it may well have been merely the result of chalk-quarrying.

A pig was roasted on a spit, another illegal activity if done without authoritative permission. Fireworks were not available with the exception of hand-held sparklers, which the other children in the party and the two of us were given. We were mainly the Redenham crowd, though there may well have been a few others from Appleshaw, although I imagine the local bobby was not necessarily informed of the event.

I tasted roast pork for the first time in my life and decided it was an improvement on green apples! The night went on forever and bedtime didn't seem to be important to the parents present, who were drinking numerous bottles of Mrs Bulwell's parsnip, elderberry and dandelion wine as well as whisky and beer brought along from the New Inn by its landlord. It was a memorable night.

CHAPTER
NINE

First Love

He stood beside our headmistress wearing a pale green shirt and shiny polished black shoes. He was staring at the floor and blushing. It was the first time I had seen a boy blush. I'd understood it to be something girls alone did. Having suffered miserably myself from the affliction for some time, my heart bled for him. He ran his fingers nervously through his thick dark hair and continued to study the floor earnestly.

My word, but he was handsome. That's how you were supposed to describe boys. They were handsome, not beautiful. Even so, at the tender age of eight I had the feeling that this was no ordinary handsome boy. His beauty was of a kind rarely seen by us at Appleshaw School. I was to discover that every girl in Standard 2 felt the same way as I did and over the next few weeks we were all to feel the sharp pain of Cupid's arrow piercing our infant hearts as fiercely as any adult might have done.

He was an evacuee. We hadn't had any at school before. Our boys were mainly those who had helped with the milking before arriving in the mornings, tousle-haired with the smell of the cowsheds ingrained in their clothes and hands callused from humping hay and silage. Even the odd one or two whose fathers didn't work on the farms scarcely merited any interest on the part of us girls. Jonnie Wells always wore a spotless white shirt and tie but when he took off his glasses he had a squint and his language was worse than anyone's and that was saying something. Country lads could teach the townies a thing or two in the way of vocabulary any day. It must have been something to do with being in close contact with all those animals so much.

But Roy, oh Roy! Even the sound of his name still has the power to make me catch my breath. I was to whisper it nightly into my pillow for the next few weeks, hugging my teddy-bear to my bosom. I wrote long letters he'd never read declaring my love and made up songs he'd never hear to sing to him.

My handsome blushing hero proved to be no softy. His skill with a ball won him star status in the eyes of the boys also and to the utter amazement of us girls, the incorporation of his personal glossary of swear words into our own resulted in virtually doubling that of the average pupil in the class.

The teacher, joy of joys, sat him in the desk across the aisle from mine. Within days I was reduced from one of the potential grammar school candidates in a couple of years time to a dithering idiot. The concentration necessary for the intricacies of the multiplication of shillings and pence, a longstanding personal quagmire, eluded me completely. I could think only of that divine profile across the gangway bent over a book and biting hard on his pencil.

There was one memorable incident when during one of my reveries I dropped my own pencil. On bending to pick it up, what should I encounter beneath the desk but the hand of my beloved gallantly attempting to retrieve it on my behalf. For one transient instant our hands met and time was suspended as we smiled at each other, our faces almost touching, a few inches from the floor between our two desks. It was the one occasion in all the time I knew him that we shared such an intimacy.

Suffering as one does at such times from the common affliction of love's blindness, it did not occur to me that my paramour had any serious failings. As a new boy uprooted from his home after witnessing the horrific scenes during the bombing of London, Roy had been spared for a week or two by our understanding teacher the daily routine of standing to read aloud to the whole class. But it was now becoming obvious that his new-found popularity was beginning to have an effect and I noticed with some slight disappointment that the blushing had become far less frequent.

The day arrived when inevitably Roy was asked to read aloud to the rest of us. We waited, the girls in the class with baited breath, to hear the now familiar and much-admired cockney vowels as Roy prepared to read his book.

The seat of his desk clanked noisily as he stood slowly and opened his copy of one of the Beacon

Readers. A faint buzz of surprise and one or two derisive sniggers rippled through the room. After all, the weakest reader in the class had long finished with those early Beacon books.

Roy's face was reddening. The blush appeared to spread from the tips of his ears down into his neck and was by the second deepening in colour until his face was almost purple.

My heart was bursting for him. Please God, help him, I prayed fervently. But it was no good. He stammered over the first word in a way barely recognisable from the manner in which we were used to hearing his voice. I breathed the first sentence in what I hoped was a whisper inaudible to the teacher. Many of us knew this book by heart for it had often fallen to us to hear the little ones practise it in the lower classes. Mercifully he must have heard me and managed to stammer the words I'd spoken. And so the tortuous process continued for the next few minutes, myself whispering a few words at a time and Roy repeating them after me. I doubt very much if there was anyone in the room who didn't realise what was going on, but no one, including the teacher, was to comment publicly on Roy's apparent illiteracy.

It stood to reason, I imagine, that his written work would be likewise flawed. Surprisingly, it appeared, his handwriting was excellent, though he could write nothing that was not copied from a book or the blackboard. In our twice-weekly dictation sessions the teacher was in the habit of awarding us twenty points in total before deducting marks for spelling mistakes and punctuation. Poor Roy was the only pupil whose total resulted in a minus figure for his first dictation, a situation I vowed would not happen again. I've often wondered what my mother made of the screwed-up scraps of Izal toilet paper she must have found in the pockets of my clothes when she came to wash them.

To my shame, I must admit to having been as a child rather contemptuous of any lack of literacy skills in my fellow pupils. Whether this was a reflection of the attitudes of adults at the time I can't say, but whatever the reason for my views concerning the weaknesses of others, as far as Roy was concerned he was totally blameless and entirely forgiven for his.

Some kind of programme must have been drawn up by the two teachers in the school to deal with Roy's problems because it was not long before there was a noticeable improvement all round. I daresay a few hundred others like him had their educational development hampered by the bombing in the cities.

There's little more to narrate of that first grand passion in my life. I was to learn much from it. I discovered for the first time how to lie and cheat in order to protect my true-love's reputation, how to suffer insults and derision in his defence and not least, the cruel truth of having to face up to the bitter pangs of jealousy. I was a skinny plain child in pigtails and unenlightened regarding relationships with boys compared with the other girls. Kiss-chase became a popular playtime game while Roy was with us. But alas, it was not in my direction the lads ran in their attempts to capture their fleeing quarry amidst squeals of delighted protest. Josephine Turner was always the boys' first choice, but she'd allow only Roy to catch her and I'd close my eyes to avoid witnessing her obvious pleasure in awarding him his prize.

Roy and his family didn't stay long in our village. One day he was not in school and the teacher told us he'd gone back to London. The whole of Standard 2 mourned his going and there were many audible sniffs from the girls.

Later in my teens I tended to have something of a penchant for youths who wore pale green shirts but never found another who was in the habit of blushing. Roy was and remains a one-off, both in my memory and in my heart.

CHAPTER
TEN

Miss Williams-Freeman

Standards 2, 3 and 4 had the privilege of being taught by the headmistress herself, whose double-barrelled surname was used only in correspondence, so to us she was just Miss Freeman.

She was a gifted teacher. Her dynamic personality and sheer enthusiasm for all the subjects on the curriculum were an inspiration to those of us who were eager to learn. Even in wartime when there must have been little money allocated for such things, every available wall-space was taken up with pictures of kings and queens, scenes of battles and historical events. Surfaces were crammed with tanks of newts and frog-spawn in season, as well as constantly replenished wild flowers with labels. And at a time when there were few books in the shops, there was even a classroom "library" ie a large bookshelf containing, judging from the illustrations, many old Victorian books which I suspect Miss Freeman had herself been responsible for collecting.

Friday afternoons were devoted to the silent reading of library books, my favourite lesson of the week. I discovered for the first time the writing of Frances

Hodgson Burnett and the story of *The Little Princess*. I learned to read fast in order to absorb as much as possible of this tale on those Friday afternoons — an acquired skill which has benefited me for the rest of my life!

Exactly what such a personality as Miss Freemen was doing in our small rural school, where I am sure few of the children were remotely interested in the subjects about which she obviously felt so passionately, is not clear. She had no family in the area and was to remain a spinster there for most of her teaching life.

Was it merely a desire to share with children her joy in the subjects she loved? If that was in fact the case, for me and for others with a similar appetite for learning, she was responsible for sowing the seeds of a lifetime's pleasure in reading and study. The fact that I ultimately chose a career in teaching I am convinced has its roots in my primary school experience. And I can appreciate that feeling of wanting to share with children the things I had myself discovered.

Miss Freeman was tall and slim with slightly-curled dark hair and prominent teeth — a feature I considered most attractive at that time. She spoke like no one else I knew, completely without an accent like those on the wireless. She loved poetry and we were constantly learning to recite poems by heart, many of which I can still remember! She read us the most gripping stories in serial form. I remember in particular *The Wind in the Willows*, the *Brer Rabbit* series and a long tale I have never managed to discover since, called *Mr Papingay's Caravan*.

Our nature lessons were most informative. My own three children were brought up having been taught the names of most of the wild flowers and trees from my memories of those endless nature walks, summer and winter alike. Sadly, my teaching has not had the same effect on them since they forgot quite quickly most of what I told them!

Bible stories, history, geography, the importance of good manners and caring for others were all absorbed into my very bones.

On reflection, as a teacher now myself, my only criticism of her might be the Friday afternoon handkerchief check! The names of those of us who did not have a hanky were noted and after three weeks of failure to produce one (in this pre-tissue era), the culprits were made to blow their noses in front of the class with the torn-off cover of an exercise book! Unfortunately, I was a frequent offender and experienced this humiliating punishment several times.

I only hope I have since lived up to half Miss Freeman's expectations of me, though I am aware that there are certain elements of my behaviour over the years that would most likely have met with her disapproval, along with her poor opinion of my nose-cleaning habits!

CHILDREN
If children live with criticism
they learn to condemn

If children live with hostility
they learn to fight
If children live with ridicule
they learn to be shy
If children live with shame
they learn to feel guilty
If children live with tolerance
they learn to be patient
If children live with encouragement
they learn confidence
If children live with praise
they learn to appreciate
If children live with fairness
they learn justice
If children live with security
they learn to have faith
If children live with approval
they learn to like themselves
If children live with acceptance and friendship
they learn to find love in the world.

(Anon).

CHAPTER
ELEVEN

The Dean's Visit

Once a year at Appleshaw School, usually in the summer, the Dean of Winchester Cathedral would pay us a visit. Catechism drill, a once-weekly feature of our school life, became an urgent daily affair in the fortnight leading up to this.

The miracles and the parables were told and retold: Jairus's daughter, The Good Samaritan, Blind Bartimaeous, The Prodigal Son, The Lame Man at the Pool of Bethesda, The Woman who touched the hem of His garment, all revolved in confusion in a mad Dervish-like dance in my brain. I was aware that the honour of the school and my beloved teacher's reputation rested on our shoulders and that it was my duty to be prepared to answer anything at all concerning the Bible.

The afternoon of the visit was preceded with much hairbrushing, handwashing and trips to the lavatories, followed by half an hour of silent reading in which we tried to compose ourselves.

Ten minutes before the Dean's expected arrival the tension was mounting intolerably. Every eye was on the open doorway. And suddenly, there he was, framed beneath the arch, God's minion himself direct from Heaven, sombre and unsmiling in his broad-brimmed black hat and cassock.

There was a clatter of hinged benches as we stood to attention beside our desks.

"Good afternoon, children," he said. "Be seated."

His head dipped a little, the better to see us above the half-moon lenses of his spectacles. Miss Freeman, hand extended in welcome, reached him in three enormous strides.

"Dean, this is indeed a pleasure. We are all ready for you, aren't we, children?" The teeth were nervously even more prominent than usual during this initial encounter.

The hat was removed from the reverend's head with utmost care and placed upon Miss Freeman's desk as a chalice upon an altar. To our astonishment the Dean seated himself, as our beloved teacher was wont to do during story-time, rather precariously upon the fender.

"Let us begin by bowing our heads in prayer."

Once more the clatter of raised benches as we stood to pray. We chanted our Lord's Prayer loudly and virtuously, if not reverently, with not an open eye to be seen.

We were tested orally, answering the Dean's questions in turn by raising our hands. We excelled ourselves that day, as I am sure we always did on the days of the Dean's visit.

A few days later six of us each received a certificate signed by the Bishop himself, confirming the fact that our knowledge of the Bible merited distinction status. The honour of the school had been upheld for yet another year.

CHAPTER TWELVE

Sunday School

The parish church of St Peter in the Wood in Appleshaw appears nowadays to be flourishing and well-attended. During the war years this was not the case. I remember going to the occasional matins service to see few people in the congregation. The elderly organist, Miss Jenkins, was proficient in accompanying the hymns for which those of us who were members of the Sunday School were expected to pump the organ bellows.

As a Church of England institution the Sunday School was not as popular as the one at the local Methodist Chapel. Marian and I were members of both! The two of us were frequently the only children at the Anglican one, with the occasional addition of a third member. Miss Jenkins, the organist, was our teacher. She was quite ancient at the time but obviously very fond of children. We learned many new hymns with her, though because lessons were in the church itself one of us was always having to work the organ bellows while the other two sang the hymns — one could not do both we discovered. She frequently invited us to tea at her cottage following our session in the church and there was always a delicious home-made cake, that even I with my odd choice of diet could not resist.

The Methodist Chapel Sunday School was completely different. There were several teachers, each having a small number of pupils grouped according to their ages, and I still have a copy of the Bible which was presented to me there in June 1941, when I would have been six years old.

Even as a child I loved the language of the Bible in spite of not understanding a lot of what I read in it! It was likewise the case with the Catechism which we knew by heart from learning it at school. I did not discover until I reached my teens the meaning of some of the commandments, for example "Thou shalt not commit adultery" and the list of things that "Thou shalt not covet", not to mention all the "begatting" in the Book of Genesis!

Marian and I were taught by Mum to say our prayers each night, which we duly did, although I had great difficulty believing that anyone was listening to me, particularly when these were expressions of "thoughts" rather than spoken words on our knees in church. Nevertheless, I had an acute sense of guilt when confronted in church by the crucifix on which the figure of Christ was evident in his loin-cloth, since I could not look at this without imagining what was underneath the draperies! I was constantly begging forgiveness in my private prayers for such sinful thoughts!

Throughout our childhood and indeed up to the ages of fifteen or sixteen when we were confirmed, Marian and I attended both church services and Sunday Schools. Having moved house several times both before and after we settled once more in Birmingham, this meant that we were for various reasons involved in a total of six or seven churches.

Mum was an ardent Anglo-Catholic, relishing the spectacular ritual of that traditional type of worship with the colourful robings of the priests, countless genuflections and swinging incense. The most memorable of this kind of service in my mind is St Oswald's church in Small Heath where my grandmother lived. Her house was directly opposite the church. I shared with my mother the love of ritual spectacle, together with the hypnotic chanting of plainsong at the services. I love it still, though I admit it is the musical and historical associations rather than any religious conviction which hold its chief attraction for me now.

I cannot escape the fact that my life is rooted in the church and its teachings, however much I try to live without it. The big Christian celebrations of Christmas and Easter are to me very much religious occasions in spite of their current overwhelming commercialisation. Music, which has been my lifetime's hobby, has always involved me in the singing and playing of religious works and the accompanying emotions which are manifest in these, both harmonically and verbally.

When we finally went back to live near Birmingham we attended briefly the local Baptist church in Shirley. Here, even at the ages of nine and eleven years, my sister and I were encouraged to sign the pledge promising not to partake of alcohol! In spite of her own views on this subject, our mother decided it was not appropriate for us and we joined the Methodists instead!

I remember well the annual Methodist Sunday School anniversaries. Marian and I, being quite competent singers, were given leading roles in these. We never forgot the two-part arrangement of "The City of Light" we sang to a packed church, performed standing on two chairs with organ accompaniment; we can sing it now!

Our ultimate allegiance, by our own choice, was to the Church of England and we finally decided to stay with our local C of E church, St James's in Shirley where we both became confirmed when we reached fifteen. When our family moved to Moseley, we were regular members at St Mary's C of E church there. As an adult I found myself in demand as an organist — or rather the "harmonium player" — at a mission church, held in a schoolroom, in the small village of Bentley Heath near Solihull. (Hard work on the knees!).

With the exception of the "happy-clappy" evangelistic category of worship, I still enjoy a traditional church service with the proviso that the music is of a reasonable standard. Which is just as well since I now have a son-in-law who is a vicar! But would I call myself a Christian? I hope that my life is based on Christian principles even though I can't honestly say that I am a convinced Christian.

CHAPTER
THIRTEEN

Farewell, Redenham

He was spoiling us, we knew that. Almost daily there would be a small gift for the two of us: a rag doll, a pencil case, a bunch of wild flowers, seeds for our own little patch of garden and fertile eggs from the market to place beneath a broody hen.

Marian could barely remember Dad from before the war. She had been less than three years old when he went away. But I, being two years older, remembered him. The memory burned like a flame in my heart for the full five years of his absence and passionate had been my nightly prayers for his safe return.

The joy of his homecoming was perpetuated for several weeks by this constant showering of gifts upon us. Each time he went out we would be waiting beneath the rose arch watching eagerly for his return with yet another prize.

The best, and as far as I can recall, the last of these were Chance and Sheba, two beautiful Golden Cocker Spaniel puppies.

It was dusk when he finally arrived home on that occasion. Bedtime had long gone, but Mum had allowed us to stay up to say goodnight to our Dad. We both knew that this time it was going to be something special. Mum had been smiling all day at nothing at all and yet had managed to shrug off our endless questions.

At the sound of footsteps on the gravel we raced to the door and down the garden path. Some instinct forbade our greeting Dad with our customary gusto and we pulled up before him holding our breath at the sight of a small bulge beneath his jacket. The care with which he reached inside to take out what was there told me at once what I hardly dared to imagine, that it was a puppy. We'd had cats before and budgies and rabbits and of course the poultry. But never a dog, though we'd often asked for one.

As I took the tiny whimpering thing into my arms, Dad drew from his jacket a second puppy and placed it against my sister's shoulder. By this time my own head was buried in the first one's warm trembling body to hide the tears I couldn't account for which were welling up in my eyes.

The puppies were not yet weaned and for a few weeks required feeding with milk from a baby's bottle. Mum, even with the privations of rationing, somehow managed to gain access to a source of out-dated Cow and Gate baby milk to feed the animals during this time. We watched with pride as their tiny bodies grew fat and strong in our care. Sheba's coat darkened in colour until at two months old it was a deep red. Chance's coat retained its pale creamy shade.

"I'm afraid Sheba will have to go," our father announced one day. "She's a bitch, you see, children," he said, taking us onto his knees and drying our tears with a large handkerchief, "and she'll want babies. We can't afford to keep any more dogs and I know someone who wants to buy her."

I was secretly glad it was Sheba who was the one to go. She was by far the better looking of the two dogs with her sleek body and beautiful colour, but it was fat, blundering, loveable Chance who had won all our hearts.

We had always known that after Dad's return at the end of the war we would be going back to Birmingham. It hadn't occurred to us how reluctant we'd feel when the time actually came. Standing beneath the arched doorway of the school, clutching my prize for doing well in the exams, I bit hard on my lip.

"I love this place," I told myself, staring out across the open fields towards the beech woods where our teacher had taken us on countless nature walks and where Chance had led us on many adventures. "It won't be the same in the town."

The excitement of the train journey made me forget my misery for a while as Marian and I made up songs to the accompaniment of the rhythm of wheels on the track.

But Chance didn't like it one bit. He cowered in the corner of the compartment and was sick. And that was not all. On the tram journey to our grandmother's house, where we were to stay until we had a place of our own to go to, Chance buried his face in the corner of a seat and trembled. Moreover, on alighting from the tram, he would allow no one to put him down onto the hard pavement. He had to be carried all the way to Grandma's by each member of the family in turn.

"He'll be alright when he gets used to the town," Mum said. But Chance never did get used to the town. He pulled on his lead and whined every time anyone attempted to take him outside the front door.

After a few weeks of this, Dad announced that he'd have to go back to live in the country. Chance's misery was so obvious and caused us all such concern that there were no tears at this decision. We could not bear to see our beloved pet so wretched. It was the only solution.

So Dad, Chance, Marian and I braved yet another train journey. It was as if Chance knew he was going home again. There was no sickness this time and his tail wagged most of the way. We watched smiling as the train screeched to a halt and the dog bounded through the open door, racing ahead of us towards where our bus would take us back to the village.

Chance's future home was to be The Iron Pear Tree, where my friend Josie Turner lived. Chance, having licked both his old and new owners half to death in his excitement made no attempt to follow us as we left the pub.

"He's happy now," Marian said, sniffing loudly.

"Yes he is, isn't he?" I added, conscious of a painful lump in my chest which wouldn't go away.

On the next and last occasion we were to see our old friend, a year or more later, he greeted us in his usual affectionate way, the familiar blundering gait somewhat hampered by his new enormous girth. His favourite haunt was now the saloon bar, we were told, where his many devoted admirers in the village frequently emptied the dregs from their beer glasses into his bowl in reward for allowing them to tickle his tummy.

"I think we did the right thing in bringing him back," Dad said as the twice-weekly bus from Andover trundled slowly and noisily along the endless country lanes towards the station.

"Yes we did," I added, aware this time more of a sense of envy than regret at parting with our old pet.

"Lucky Chance," said Marian.

"Lucky Chance," I echoed.

It was good once more to be near all the cousins on our return to Birmingham and I particularly loved my Grandma's company, a relationship that was to be a close one right up to the time of her death at ninety-two years of age. I was so glad she was around to attend my wedding. She was the only member of the family to completely accept my husband. I believe that may have had something to do with the fact that she appreciated he didn't make me pregnant for the first four years of our marriage! Unfortunately that also meant that she did not live long enough to see any of my children, though cousin Tony had already presented her with her first great-grandchild.

Marian and I missed the freedom we'd enjoyed when living in the country. In those early days of being in the city, apart from trips to Small Heath park where we used to fish for tiddlers and collect frog spawn, our mother was nervous of allowing us to catch buses or wander too far from home. I think we both felt rather like poor Chance, slightly out of place in this new environment of busy roads, noise and hard pavements. Even when we eventually moved to Solihull, although a great improvement on Small Heath, it could not compare with our old lifestyle, living in rural Hampshire.

I missed the constant murmur of chickens beneath the kitchen window, the chatter of rooks overhead in their endless evening flight, the rustle of the cornfields and even the noisy splatter of rain on the bungalow's galvanised roof. I missed seeing Grandpa Morrell in his panama hat, chipping spars for thatching as he sat on a hay bale at the end of the lane, where we passed him each day on the way home from school. These sights and sounds of my childhood created a permanent impression on my mind, even though I may have been unaware of it at the time.

There were a few weeks spent at a local school in Small Heath before we moved to Solihull. I had been there briefly on a previous visit to my grandmother's when I had stayed on with her a year earlier, following a Christmas spent there with the family. Unlike the hostile atmosphere I experienced the following term at the Solihull primary school, I quite enjoyed those two short periods at St Benedict's Road in Small Heath.

The class teacher's own specialist subject appeared to be art, and although I never had any particular talent for the subject, I remember well how when I was trying to draw a pig, she made me look closely at a picture of the animal's hind quarters. My final painting, of which I was extremely proud, was displayed on a special board in the assembly hall. In my later school life I was never to come across another teacher able to communicate to me the ability to draw anything else, but I can still make a fair effort at pigs!

Likewise, in spite of the brevity of the time spent at St Benedict's, I was to enjoy some exciting new music. This was obviously the headmaster's subject and each week he would take the whole school for some inspirational singing lessons. I remember learning Parry's "Jerusalem", Mendelssohn's "On Wings of Song" and one or two of the more rousing hymns from the "Songs of Praise" hymn book.

The anticipation of the move to Solihull was more enjoyable than the reality of it. Our new home was to be a three-bedroomed semi in Shirley, about three miles from my new grammar school, which, for reasons I'll explain later, I was not to attend for another year.

The previous owners had given the house a name, identified by a sign on the front door: "Tranquil"! I have a suspicion our mother chose the house deliberately on account of this name! She took pains to explain to us exactly what the word meant and assured us our new life there would be influenced simply because of it! I don't think this was exactly borne out when it came to it, though we all loved the house, which both Marian and I appreciated, belonged to us and not to a landlord. There was even a greenhouse for Dad that enabled him to make the garden really special with his displays of chrysanthemums and dahlias. He also managed to grow tomatoes and cucumbers in the greenhouse, which kept Mum happy!

But those memories of Redenham: the endless stretch of open fields, standing beneath the rose arch watching the sun set, plucking apples from trees when we were hungry and just running wild when and wherever we felt like it, were to remain in our hearts. This had been for us as children, if not for our mother, an ideal world to re-live in our dreams for the rest of our lives.

CHAPTER
FOURTEEN

Mother

Marion Thomas (daughter Marian was named after her with slightly altered spelling) was the fourth of eight children born to Annie Clara, who had two full-term still-births following these. Charlie, the second child, was killed at the age of five in a road accident before Marion's birth, mown down by a horse and cart.

Annie Clara's husband, Joseph, was a professional soldier who fought and was severely wounded in the Boer wars at the beginning of the 20th century. Although he possessed certain mechanical skills, he was never able to hold down a job using them for any length of time once he was discharged from the army. For long periods he was unable to work as a result of his war-wound and received a pittance in the way of a disability army pension, certainly not enough to keep his family of a wife and seven children.

As the first of her eight grandchildren, I was to hear at first hand from my grandmother the "romantic" tale of her elopement at the age of eighteen, with her soldier-husband, who was several years her senior. She was a Coventry weaver at the time and married against the wishes of her parents, who she told me she did not see again after her marriage.

I think the truth was probably a little different from the version I heard from her. As an eighteen-year-old she would not then have been allowed to marry without her parents' permission, which would account for the facts I later discovered on tracing the family history. Her marriage certificate notes that she was actually married at the age of twenty-two, but her address for the intervening few years is different from the one where her parents were living. This would have been very unusual for a young working-class girl at the time, unless she was in fact living at the same address as her future husband. Doubtless quite scandalous behaviour for the period, I imagine. It beggars belief that this was actually the case, since I only ever knew my grandmother as the most straight-laced, morally correct of characters. Nevertheless, love was most likely blind to all the possible consequences of her actions at the time. Did she ever live to regret her decision, I wonder? After undergoing childbirth a total of ten times and a lifetime spent in abject poverty, maybe she came to wish she had considered the advice of her parents!

My grandfather, whom I never knew since he died long before I was born, was a typical Victorian "master of the house". Mealtimes were conducted in absolute silence and children were not permitted to leave any food on their plates. My mother was in the habit of secretly pocketing scraps from her sisters' meals since she was always hungry whilst they were rarely so. (Two of my aunts were always skinny, living into their nineties on very little food!). In spite of the fact that he did not earn enough money for his family to live on, Grandfather had the reputation of being frequently drunk. Admittedly alcohol was notoriously cheap at that time and he might be excused somewhat, finding his situation in life intolerable as a result of not being able to earn a fitting wage.

Nevertheless my mother idolised her father and claimed to have had a special relationship with him. It was she who was regularly sent by Grandma to fetch him home from the pub, where he enjoyed being something of a local celebrity, telling of his exploits in the army: how he saved the life of his commanding officer from the spear of a Zulu warrior and other tales.

Our mother always felt she was the odd one out of the four girls, her three sisters being intellectually her superiors. In a later age they would most surely have gone on to higher education and study at university, but this was not possible in their family's financial climate at the time. Even so, once they were earning, two of them pursued evening classes in French and the third acquired shorthand and typing skills. Mum found her brothers easier company than her sisters.

Being extremely good-looking and several times requested by photographers for her portrait (at no cost) to display in their shop windows, as well as being her father's favourite, may possibly have been the cause of some jealousy among the sisters. Although she was not the eldest, Marion, never short of gentlemen friends, was the first of the girls to marry.

Without the benefit of any special education, the three boys left school at 14 to work in factories. Grandma had to take in washing to eke out the family income and the girls before leaving school were involved in helping out with the ironing, deliveries of linen and general housework. Anne, the youngest of the family, had had polio at the age of five years and with her consequential disability, a permanent very serious limp, was excused much of this sort of work. Marion also contributed a few pence each week washing dishes for neighbours. Life was hard.

Grandfather died at the age of 45 years. Grandma survived him by a further 47 years. There is a particularly revealing story regarding Grandfather's death which I think illustrates significantly Grandma's attitude to the important business of family income.

Grandfather had become bedridden towards the end of his life and was therefore sleeping downstairs. Daughter Anne, since her polio illness, was also sleeping downstairs. Marion, to ease these night-time arrangements, had lately been staying with neighbours, who were a particularly musical family with no children of their own. She would sing for them to the accompaniment of their piano, which was mutually enjoyable both for her and for them.

Marion, aged twenty at the time, was in the habit of calling in to see her father every morning before going to work at Lucas's factory. One Friday morning she called in as usual and was told by her mother not to disturb her father since he was sleeping. She went to work and called instead on the way home. She had a premonition on her return, seeing that all the curtains in the road were drawn, that something had happened.

To her surprise and dismay, she discovered that her father had in fact died the previous night, although her mother had decided not to tell her this because the following day happened to be a Friday, the day she was to receive her wages from the factory. Marion's wages were obviously of far more importance to her mother than was imparting the news of her father's death, presumably because if she had known about it she would most likely have not gone into the factory to collect her money, as indeed had been the case with her brothers who had been present in the house when their father died.

Marion never forgave her mother for this. It was a tale she would tell us, her daughters, many times. We always understood that our mother's relationship with her father was far more important to her than that with her mother.

All four sisters were musical, the youngest, Anne, being a competent piano accompanist for Marion, whose contralto voice won her considerable acclaim at local social functions. In the early days of her marriage to our father she was a member of a concert party earning a wage for her singing. My arrival nine months after the wedding put paid to this as a possible career for her.

Mum's singing became a background accompaniment to our childhood. At home the simplest remark would prompt an echo in song. Although both my sister and I, on reaching secondary school age, eventually learned to play the piano to a reasonable standard, having been given an instrument by a fond aunt, I have always regretted that we did not acquire one earlier. I am sure it would have benefited the family during those long winter evenings in Redenham during the war. Our mother, like her sisters, had studied the piano, mainly as a means of helping her to learn songs for her singing lessons.

As it was, Mum did her best to entertain us, mainly with stories. She used to travel as far away as Salisbury in order to attend the outdoor market held there at weekends. On her return each time she would be weighed down with bags of cheap vegetables and parcels of second-hand books in string-tied bundles.

The books were chiefly Victorian tales of misunderstood, frequently orphaned, heroines, whose selfless deeds changed lives and brought honour and prestige to all who befriended them. The two of us would sit around our mother before the kitchen range, weeping silently into our hankies, Mum's tears shed maybe for personal reasons often accompanying ours. I remember in particular "Theodora" (her name means God's gift!) and Dorothy's Trust.

Apart from the ones bought from Salisbury market and a regular supply of Rupert Bear Annuals sent each Christmas by an uncle, I remember owning only one other book: a large illustrated collection of Hans Andersen Fairy Tales. Together with encyclopaedias borrowed from Mr Pound's library, we were therefore well supplied with reading material, which I am sure contributed considerably towards our intellectual development.

Our mother was aware of this need and although she herself had had little more than the standard schooling of her day to the age of fourteen, was determined to ensure that her daughters would have the utmost educational opportunities denied to herself. My sister Marian and I were lucky to benefit from the new Education Act of 1944, which enabled us both to attain a free grammar school place after passing the eleven-plus examination.

Since ours was the only branch of Mum's family at that time to venture beyond the bounds of the City of Birmingham, it was not surprising that we had a constant stream of visitors to our country bungalow. Seaside holidays, infrequent as they were for working-class families, became non-existent in wartime. I remember one trip we made to Bournemouth only to find the whole stretch of beaches there cordoned off with large coils of barbed wire and notices forbidding access to any part of the sea-front. For Mum's brothers and sisters our home was a welcome alternative for their occasional work-breaks, even though none of them, apart from Aunt Anne, at that time had cars and the journey by train was not easy.

It meant that Marian and I became very close to our three eldest cousins, whom we grew up to regard virtually as siblings. In addition, all of us spent most Christmases together at Grandma's house in Birmingham, with all the traditional Victorian activities of charades, play-acting, singing carols round the tree, silver threepenny-pieces in the pudding and the frenzied preparations for Santa's visit. At lunchtime there would be the traditional family toast to the two absentees, our Dad and Aunt Winnie, one of Mum's sisters who was living as a nanny in Paris and who, following a dramatic escape from her internment camp, worked for the French Resistance.

Although they remained together for the rest of their lives, I don't regard my parents' marriage as a particularly happy one. Dad could never share Mum's interest in her music and I don't remember him ever attending any of the concerts she sang in after the war. Likewise, his passion for growing flowers (he always kept a beautiful garden and won prizes at flower shows for his chrysanthemums and dahlias) was not something she could appreciate either. She constantly criticised him for not growing vegetables instead, for which he had not the remotest interest!

Nevertheless, we seemed to live a fairly typical working-class family life for that era, never having quite enough money (our school uniforms were always bought second-hand) and Mum having to do spells of clerical work from time to time to keep the bills and the mortgage premiums paid. The job she held for the longest time was that of a school meals supervisor (we later called them "dinner nannies"), which paid very little but which Mum enjoyed doing. None of my friends' mothers worked, with the exception of one girl whose mother was a widow and also a qualified teacher.

Dad was too old and unfit for the army after the war. On purchasing a house in Solihull he found a position locally growing chrysanthemums at Woolman's Nurseries. The wages then paid for this kind of work were abysmally low but he loved it. However, it became essential after a few years for him to find work in a factory, which made him very unhappy. The lack of a sufficient income was something that worried Mum far more than Dad, whose happy-go-lucky attitude to life was a delightful part of his character but which made him a constant victim of Mum's henpecking.

Unlike Dad, Mum had an overriding ambition in life that he did not share. It had little to do with the immediate problems of how to grow the next prize-winning bloom or even how to pay the latest bill. Her courage in the perseverance of her belief that it was possible to ensure a brighter future for the next and possibly further generations of the family was remarkable. She faced life head-on to this end, whatever the challenges: war, poverty, loneliness and the general unfairness of life on the lower echelons of the class system.

It is our mother that young Marian and I have to thank for making sure that we would not necessarily be dependent solely on a husband's income. In spite of her fears, we were both lucky in making good and lasting marriages, but we had had the background of a good education and training for a profession, which considerably enhanced both our lives.

Mother was a strong character, though maybe not as clever as her sisters, whose ambition won through in the end. After her death, by which time we were both adults with our own families, my sister summed up the feelings of both of us with the remark, "It's her strength I miss,"

And it is still, thirty years on.

A SILK PICTURE
Click clack, click clack.
the heddles separate the warp threads
ceaselessly, noisily,
to let the shuttle through.
It echoes in her brain,
"Shall I? Shan't I? Shall I? Shan't I?"

Click clack, click clack.
The pattern on the silk grows:
red roses on a white background,
burgeoning
like the love within her heart.
The regiment will be gone next week
to Africa;
she must decide.

Click clack, click clack.
The bobbins spin as weft on warp
completes the final petals,
and there are no more roses,
just a band of white.

Click clack, click clack.
The picture's clearer now.
It is her life arrayed there
on the loom.
And the choice is made for her.

*Fay Garrison, prize-winning entry for a
Coventry Libraries poetry competition, 1990,
written in memory of
Grandmother Annie Clara Thomas.*

CHAPTER
FIFTEEN

Aunts and Uncles

My father, John Lee, was the youngest of three children. He had two older sisters, Lily and Elsie. I can't remember visiting them more than half a dozen times when we were children. My mother's family, and indeed my mother herself, were of the opinion that they were not socially in the same class as the Thomas family, though why this should have been the case escapes me! It may have had something to do with the fact that my paternal grandmother had a reputation for frequently over-indulging in the drinking of gin.

Dad did not speak of this very often, but his relationship with his mother was obviously not a close one. When he did talk about his childhood we understood it to be have been one of extreme hardship at the time of the depression in Birmingham before and during the first world war until he joined the army aged sixteen. He told us he often went barefoot as a child and rarely had enough food to eat except what he could scavenge from neighbours. He never actually said that this was due to the fact that his mother was frequently drunk, but that is what we assumed on hearing these tales. She died in her sixties just after the war ended and Dad made a significantly positive decision not to attend her funeral! No reason for this was ever given to us as children nor even later in our lives. It was a subject we were led to believe was never to be mentioned at any time.

But Dad did love his sisters, particularly the elder one, Lily. She had an exceptionally happy marriage and was the mother of thirteen children! They only ever lived in the slums of Aston, Birmingham, and although Aunt Lily was rather self-conscious about the number of children she'd had, I don't remember her ever regretting the fact that she'd had them! I got to know the family much better in my teens and attended the occasional weddings of my cousins.

It was a completely different story with my mother's family. Even with the differences between herself and her sisters, which were never completely resolved right up to her death (Mum was the first of the girls to die), our family was always very involved with Mum's siblings. All the brothers and sisters alike, were extremely fond of little Marian and myself. I think it had something to do with the fact that we were both girls as well as being two of the older grandchildren.

I adored my Aunts, often staying with them on my own in the years before they married. Aunt Winnie did not in fact marry (she was engaged three times, she told us!) but I stayed with her in Paris along with my cousin John when we were both eleven years old. We never tired of the tales of her life in two internment camps, the notorious Besancon and later Vittel, and her subsequent escape and work with the Resistance.

With the aid of the Resistance movement she returned to England in 1943, along with the three little girls of the Ory family she'd been caring for before the occupation of Paris and whose father was imprisoned in Dachau, in spite of the fact that he was a devout Roman Catholic businessman and not Jewish at all.

The dramatic story of Winnie's escape from the internment camp became headline news in the Birmingham Post, which described her as "The Girl Pimpernel", since she had herself negotiated the escape of several Jewish women from the Vittel camp.

The three Ory sisters, Winnie's charges, spent the remainder of the war and a few years afterwards in Birmingham. We were to become good friends with them. The girls' mother, Winnie told us, was devoted to her husband, and spent much of the time, whilst her children were in England, nursing him back to health in Paris following his release from the concentration camp at the end of the war. Winnie's description of the reunion of Monsieur and Madame Ory at Gare St Lazare on his return, which I understand was witnessed by her, was extremely moving. Monsieur Ory stepped from the train, it appears, clad in nothing more than a blanket, with a close-shaven head and only one tooth, whereupon his wife cradled him in her arms and kissed him long and ardently.

Madame Ory's nursing care was well-rewarded in that the two of them both lived well into their eighties and presumably had a fairly normal life thereafter. The eldest daughter, however, told us only recently that they always regarded Winnie as their main guardian since she was the one who, apart from two years of her internment, was always with them until they reached secondary school age and was never far away even after she left the family to work with another. In fact she became nanny to Françoise Ory's two daughters several years later.

Since neither the Orys nor daughter Françoise's family were particularly wealthy, I imagine quite a lot of Winnie's work with them was done for little reward, except that I know she always thought of the children as her own. And like her Thomas sisters, she was brilliant with money! I understand that alongside looking after children when they were back in Paris, she spent time whilst they were at school teaching English. Among her pupils were the children of the Rothschild family, who also spent summer holidays at her house near Bournemouth in Dorset, an area where all the Thomas sisters had eventually decided to make their homes in the fifties and sixties. Winnie also set herself up as an exchange agent, organising holidays and English-speaking courses for French children with her sisters and other people she knew in the South of England.

Aunt Winnie has already become something of a legend in the Thomas ancestral archives. Attendance at her funeral a few years ago (she died aged 97, the last of the Thomas siblings) included several of her old French charges from two generations! She had been responsible for the upbringing, she told us, of twenty-five babies!

Aunt Flo (Florence Amelia Nightingale Thomas — her father's name choice!), was the eldest of the sisters, Annie Clara's third child, born after Charlie, the one who was to die in a road accident aged five. Aunt Flo and I had a very special relationship for the duration of her life. It was understood her ambition was to have a daughter like me. She married quite late and was to have just one son two years after my birth. My cousin Tony says he was never forgiven for not being a girl!

Anne was the youngest member of the family, there being ten years between herself and her eldest sister Flo. Anne's disability following her polio illness at the age of five years had little noticeable effect on her lifestyle, including her choice of career, at a time when this might possibly have been unusual. She was the first person, male or female, in the family to own a car. Hers was the only car in which we ever experienced being driven for most of our childhood.

Having been told she would never be able to have children because of her disability, Anne made a great fuss of me, the first of her three nieces. If my sister had been more of an extrovert, maybe she would have been included in this close relationship, but she was always loath to leave Mum for any length of time. Anne was a very independent person who owned her own house and even negotiated the purchase in addition of the house her widowed mother was renting. Like her two sisters, Winnie and our mother, she was incredibly clever in the management of money.

Anne worked for many years as a shorthand typist at The Woodlands Hospital in Birmingham. On my frequent visits to stay with her I was often taken along to the hospital and remember frequently sitting under her desk reading a book, something Health and Safety regulations certainly would not tolerate in this day and age.

She was a charismatic and quite beautiful young lady with an infectious sense of humour, whose disability was scarcely noticeable within minutes of her company. I used to love watching her brush her long golden-blond hair with a wire hairbrush the traditional hundred strokes a time and setting it daily in the Lady-Jayne metal wave-making clips before fastening it at the back of her head in a kind of French pleat or bun.

There were several "gentlemen-friends" (the term "boyfriend" was not then used) in attendance during the years I was my aunt's young companion. I was told to call them "Uncle". Once I accompanied Aunt Anne to Sunday lunch at the home of Uncle Cyril's family and was quite overwhelmed at the grandeur of the occasion. The marble fireplaces, high ceilings and gold-framed portrait-covered walls, not to mention the starched table linen, beautiful porcelain and silver cutlery, took my breath away. So much so that when it came to attempting to eat the soggy half-cooked offering I was informed was "Yorkshire pudding", so different from the crispy delicious version my mother baked at home, I seriously risked being sick into my beautiful linen napkin rather than leave it on my plate, having always understood that it was bad manners to do so! This was not the place for the tolerance of bad manners, I felt! I understood (from Mum) that the relationship with Uncle Cyril, although quite a long one, ended because of his fondness for alcohol, something of which their family had already had experience.

In her forties, following a late marriage, Anne amazed everyone (including her doctor!) by having two children by Caesarean Section within twelve months of each other. In spite of the age gap of sixteen years and more, Marian and I have always been remarkably close to our younger cousins.

Having lived in married quarters in the early days of her marriage, our mother learned that it was possible, even for people in their walk of life, to buy property by way of a mortgage loan. With the help of a couple of her siblings she managed to borrow the necessary twenty-five pounds deposit for a new bungalow in Gosport in the South of England where Dad was stationed at the time they married. Dad was moved around several times before the war and therefore the bungalow had to be sold, but Mum's nest-egg was added to over the years so that when we were eventually able to settle in Birmingham we had enough money to buy a house.

The three brothers were frequent visitors and I loved my cousin John, Jack's son, who was the same age as me and was my first sweetheart. We had similar tastes, were both avid classical music lovers and were in our teens and twenties members of the same amateur operatic society. The friendship lasted until our respective marriages, when we lost touch with each other for a long time. His early death at fifty was the first one of our generation. He is still sorely missed.

In spite of the rest of the Thomas family's life-long political Conservative persuasion, Uncle Jack was a staunch Communist and strong Union man at The Rover factory in Solihull during the notorious period in the fifties and sixties when the unions were all-powerful. As a shop-steward I daresay he played a significant part in the strikes at that time, much to the chagrin of his siblings.

The youngest of the brothers, Jim, also worked in a Birmingham factory until his death in his early sixties. His wife, another Flo, for some reason always known as Aunt Lolly, was a successful athlete at Birchfield Harriers and held several Midland Walking Championship medals. She had one child in her forties, our youngest cousin David, bringing the total number of our generation of Thomases to eight.

I continued regularly to visit Uncle Joe and Aunt Gertrude, my god-parents, who lived not far from us in Solihull, until the time of my marriage. Their post-war semi, though a fairly modern building when viewed from the outside, was transformed into something of a time-warp when one entered the house. A television set did put in an appearance for a few months, but was despatched to the garden shed once Aunt Gertrude decided some of the programmes were too indecent to be viewed in her living room! No central heating was ever installed (even though this was in the seventies) and in spite of having two taps over the ceramic sink in the kitchen, there was no immersion heater either. All water had to be boiled in a kettle on the gas stove, which for their weekly baths meant being carried upstairs in saucepans! It is no surprise that the end of both their lives, in their eighties, came about as the result of accidents! Aunt Gertrude's followed a fall, the anxiety about which when rushing to get help caused Uncle Joe to have a stroke. Luckily a good neighbour became aware that there was a problem and called the police, who got them both to hospital. After Gertrude's death Uncle Joe was taken to live with his sister Anne, who had by then moved to The New Forest not far from our widowed mother. Although quite frail, he managed to live to the age of eighty-three.

There were the inevitable family quarrels over money and disputed wills, although our remarkable Aunt Winnie, only too aware of these things, made it her business to ensure this would not be the case when she died. As one with no children of her own, she consulted solicitors and made a very clear will naming her remaining seven nieces and nephews as her beneficiaries. Since she lived to the age of ninety-seven and spent her last two years with dementia in a nursing home, this turned out to be a wise decision on her part!

The remaining family, our own generation, now spread across the country and indeed the globe, used to meet up fairly regularly in order to attend the funerals of the old folk. Latterly, as we ourselves hover around our sixties and seventies, we tend to gather together periodically in order to attend one another's significant birthdays.

The Thomas family ties are still there even though we are a truly diverse bunch of characters.

CHAPTER SIXTEEN

Growing Up

My memory of the time we lived in Redenham remains very clear and in much greater detail than what happened in later years. The contrast between city life and that in the country could not have been more different. However, that may also have had something to do with the fact that we had Dad at home after the war, and therefore our parents' volatile relationship may have influenced our lives in a way which did not apply when we were living in Redenham.

I never quite came to terms with the inconsistent behaviour of our mother, comparing her apparent solicitude and regret at the absence of her husband during the time he was away with her dismissive indifference when he was at home!

There was a brief "honeymoon" period at first, during which time Dad was obviously not well. Five years of imprisonment dreaming of the food he would eat on his release took some time to be realised. On taking a bite of his first pork chop he was sick. Following a diet of watery soup with black stale bread and potato peelings (his description of the prison food), he was unable for some time to eat normally and remained gaunt and weak for several months. The Red Cross parcels received by the prisoners had been life-savers, he told us. At least there had been the occasional mug of tea and some sugar.

Both Mum and Dad, having suffered in their youth from having a parent who over-indulged in the imbibing of alcohol, neither of them ever drank any except for a bottle of sherry at Christmas. I never knew them to enter a pub even once in their lives!

Tea became an important ingredient in their daily life. There seemed always to be a pot of fresh tea on the kitchen table. No one made it quite like my Dad. To this day I am unable to replicate his tea. I think it must have been something he learned to do par excellence in India, where he spent his first few years in the army. (No tea-bags, naturally!)

On our return to Birmingham we lived at first in a rented house a few doors from Grandma Thomas in Small Heath, but it was only a short time before we bought a semi-detached house of our own in Solihull, a rather up-market area noted for its fashionable society and good schools. Unfortunately this fact was reflected in the cost of the new school uniform I needed when moving into the grammar school some time later. This cost, happily for our family finances at the time, was delayed by a year because the grammar school to which I had been allocated was over-subscribed, the new buildings scheduled to be in place for the increased intake that year not being ready. Thirty or so potential pupils, myself included, were transferred to a local secondary modern school for the first twelve months of our secondary education. The class remained together and was referred to as "the grammar school annexe", moving en masse to the new school the following year.

I must admit, I consider our group to have been the lucky ones, enjoying some of the best teaching in that "annexe" year that I was to encounter during the whole of my secondary school life! I remember the subject of mathematics in particular, this being the subject which had always been a nightmare for me personally. Suddenly, even with the introduction of geometry and algebra, I began to see some daylight in what had been a mere jumble of figures for several years. I even came second in the end-of-year geometry exam! Unfortunately, on transferring to the grammar school, in spite of streaming, I managed to relapse once more, eventually having to take the maths O-level exam a total of three times before I passed it in order to qualify for entry into a teacher training college!

Mum drained the family coffers in order that I should have a new blazer on starting the new school, but everything else had to be bought secondhand. At that time this fact was not something I was eager for my fellow pupils to know about when questioned as to the difference in the shade of brown between their gymslips and mine! Likewise when it came to paying up front for a whole term of school dinners, Mum had to borrow money from one of her sisters! She was now, of course, also having to pay mortgage premiums on top of everything else.

Dad had continued to receive his army pay for a few months after his return following the war, until he began working at Woolman's chrysanthemum nurseries when we moved to Solihull. It was always Mum who was in charge of the family money. In fact I don't believe my dad ever held a bank account! He appeared to be perfectly happy about this situation.

So here we were, having chosen to live in one of the more prestigious areas in the midlands, despite our straitened circumstances. It was something I was never completely able to come to terms with during the whole of my school life, being perpetually aware that our family was not like the other girls' families. I remember once being acutely embarrassed whilst entertaining a few friends to tea on the occasion of my birthday, when my father arrived home from the nurseries on his bike, clad in his scruffy working clothes, which understandably, given the nature of his job, were covered in mud.

Of course I have since become aware that I was not the only pupil to feel self-conscious in this way about her family circumstances. I discovered some years later that there were several girls who felt exactly as I did concerning their comparatively lowly financial status in those years following the free school places scheme. The fact that Malvern Hall High School for Girls had only a couple of years before my arrival been an all-fee-paying private school (and presumably was still charging fees for those pupils) meant that the older girls had a background far different from my own.

Luckily, apart from the subject of mathematics, I was to fare quite well academically in those early years at the new school. For some reason I blossomed in the new subject of French — probably something to do with the fact that Aunt Winnie lived in France and I desperately wanted to learn the language. Up to the O-level exam in the subject I found myself, even in the A stream, able to come top in all the French exams. On beginning Latin a similar thing happened. However, for one reason or another, my early promise was never fulfilled when it came to the important time of O-levels. I suspect the common teenager's emotional crises began to affect my performance at those particular exam times.

The close relationship I'd had with Dad as a small girl continued well into my teens and was always a much easier one than that with my mother. The teenage years with Mum were difficult. During study in the subject of psychology during my teacher-training, I attempted to analyse these problems, coming to the conclusion that on my own part they stemmed from the time I had been sent away to live with Mum's brother and his wife following my illness at the age of four-going-on-five. The fear of rejection, although not realised at the time, never completely left me and was to affect other relationships I would encounter in later years, including that with my husband. Equally, the fact that Mum was not an easy character anyway, something borne out by her own relationships with her mother, her sisters and even little Marian (who was much closer to her than I was), meant that at times the atmosphere was frenzied.

Nevertheless, maybe even because of these difficulties, the effect on me of her eventual death some years later was devastating. Was this possibly the ultimate rejection?

Not having any brothers, I tended to avoid the subject of boyfriends until I reached my late teens. I was intrigued to hear the tales of those girls who did mix with the opposite sex, but was nervous of doing so myself, probably influenced by our mother who positively discouraged it. I was nevertheless quite flattered on hearing from a girl in my class that I was the object of a strong infatuation by the charismatic son of my piano teacher for whom she acquired the gift of a portrait of me drawn by another classmate! I was almost sixteen at the time and had recently had my pigtails removed!

Inevitably, with hormones affecting one as is usual at this age, there had to be some kind of outlet for the frustrated emotions lurking in my breast. With no males on the horizon, this meant that the object of my affections would have to be another girl. It was quite common in those days of one-sex schools for the younger girls to acquire "crushes" or "pashes" on older girls, prefects or teachers (who were likewise all female!). These were unlikely to develop into what we now recognise as lesbian relationships — a subject at that time about which we knew nothing. But the feelings involved were nevertheless very strong and could sometimes be disturbing. Most of my friends had these attachments, occasionally for two or three prefects at a time who were frequently adored for their physical prowess on the games field, a typical male-type quality! They tended to be, like myself, from all-female families who were not in the habit of encountering young males in their daily lives.

The object of my passion was Barbara, my head of table at lunch times, an appointment given to sixth-formers who would have about seven younger girls from the same house allotted to her dining table. The main attraction for me was that she was a first-class pianist, in the process of studying for her Grade VIII piano exam. Music had by now become the overall love of my life and even with our restricted financial resources, I had begun to acquire a collection of classical records, encouraged by our mother who herself rated the subject highly.

My best friend, Anne, on the same table as me, was equally smitten with Barbara and like me she was a classical music fanatic. To our great delight we found ourselves attending the same concerts as Barbara at the Birmingham Town Hall — these were usually a series of "Youth Concerts" or "The Birmingham Proms", with special cheap-rate tickets for which we needed to save up our meagre pocket money.

Unlike Anne, I was something of an extrovert and was not satisfied with admiring the object of my desire from a distance. I was determined to make a friend of Barbara, which was not easy since she was two years my senior, at that age something of a problem. I nevertheless managed to do this and the two of us began going to concerts together.

By the time I reached the summer of O-levels in 1951 (this was the first year of the change from the exams previously labelled "School Certificate"), my emotions were in turmoil and my relationship with my mother was at its worst! Barbara was about to leave school to go to Teacher Training College and our family had moved to Moseley, a seven-mile journey from Solihull which Marian and I negotiated daily on our new bicycles.

We were now living in a seven-bedroomed double-fronted Victorian mansion in Moseley, with the impressive name of "Hango Mount", purchased at the same price as that we had received for the sale of our semi in Solihull! Taste for this kind of property was later to change considerably but it was not popular at the time, hence the comparatively low price. My parents were to turn it into a bed and breakfast boarding house, letting out at least four of the bedrooms.

Together with the fact that Dad had left Woolman's nurseries and was working at the Territorial Army Headquarters earning more money, this was the making of us financially. We suddenly had money to spare for new school uniforms, the bicycles, a new piano (we'd hitherto had only a mini-piano with a shortened keyboard) and trips to as many concerts as I wanted. We also bought our first car, Dad having first to learn to drive it and having to take the driving test three times before he succeeded in passing it, despite his having ridden a motor bike for most of his army career!

But my sister and I hated our new life! We were embarrassingly conscious that other people at school did not have to share their home with strangers and we were reluctant to bring friends home who might witness this fact. It is obviously something in this day and age which would be perfectly acceptable to anyone, but the class distinctions at the time were very strictly defined. Mum and Dad endured our obvious displeasure and at times downright misery for a few years, which included some dire results for my O-levels, before deciding to return to Solihull and life once more in a semi.

My sister's O-level results two years after mine plus my own A-levels reflected our complete about-turn and comfortable acceptance of life back in Solihull, even though Mum continued now and then to take in the odd couple of lodgers for short periods.

My relationship with Barbara continued well into her college years and even my own two years later. We corresponded regularly, sharing a mutual passion for the subject of music in a way I would not do again until meeting my husband, a superb violinist and music graduate whose life was equally as devoted to the subject as my own.

Although Barbara and I attended one another's weddings, we lost touch following the births of our children (we both had two girls and a boy within two years of each other). A few years ago, having moved away from the Midlands to live near one of my daughters following my husband's death, I hosted a huge gathering of relatives and old school friends at my seventieth birthday party. I was by that time completely unable to contact Barbara, which I regret. We have both moved around the country a number of times in connection with our husbands' professional careers and consequently lost touch with our mutual contacts. Having had a number of serious health problems of my own as I grew older, I sometimes wonder if she may possibly no longer be alive.

In the now enlightened climate of information regarding same-sex relationships, I realise that our friendship was completely innocent of any sexual behaviour beyond the usual girly demonstrations of the odd kiss and occasional hand-holding. Nevertheless, my own feelings concerning her and the sharing of our love for music has been an important part of my development.

I was to attend teacher training college for two years after I left school, returning to Solihull to live with my parents again (big mistake!) and to teach in a local school for the next five years before my marriage to Victor Garrison.

CHAPTER
SEVENTEEN

Music and Marriage

If I had been fond of music before attending Malvern Hall High School for Girls it was soon to become the overriding passion in my life. The school had been blessed with the most gifted and inspiring music teacher it was possible to encounter. Margaret Wharam was to teach there for the whole of her career and apart from a few individual instrumental teachers, did the job without assistance.

Following a period when it became a mixed comprehensive (to Miss Wharam's disgust!), Malvern Hall, the subject of Constable's famous painting, was eventually sold by the local authority to become a girls' private school, by which time it had enjoyed over thirty years as a grammar school. Scores of letters have appeared over those years in the annual school magazines bearing testimony to the fact that past pupils' lives had been transformed by the music teaching experienced there at the hands of Margaret Wharam. And yet, as my husband, who was involved in teacher-training, was to comment when he came to know her, so unorthodox were her ideas and teaching methods, it was questionable she'd have in his day passed any education tutor's list of qualities required to qualify for the profession! I can remember her once very angrily giving a girl an "order mark" for saying she thought Handel's music was "boring"!

There were a vast number of pupils like me over the years, who, thanks to Margaret Wharam, found themselves stimulated by the works of Bach in particular, along with most of the other great composers. Her sheer joy in and enthusiasm for the music she loved she somehow managed to transfer to us all.

Quite recently, having moved away from the central midlands some years ago, I found myself, whilst rehearsing the B Minor Mass in the Nottingham Bach Choir, exchanging eulogies with a fellow choir member concerning our respective school music teachers who had introduced us to Bach. It was not until the end of the rehearsal that we suddenly discovered we'd been talking about the same person and that we'd both attended Malvern Hall School within a few years of each other! This was, I imagine, not so much a coincidence as an inevitability; after all it's quite likely that many of Miss Wharam's ex-pupils should find themselves singing in a "Bach Choir" in whichever part of the country they might choose to live.

During the years before I married I continued to be very involved in the local music scene in Solihull, most of which tended to be run by Margaret Wharam. She even persuaded me to become something of a solo singer, which had never been the case when I was a schoolgirl. I began to take on lead roles in the Gilbert and Sullivan Operatic Society and to give the occasional recital at local amateur concerts. When Margaret's (adult) Solihull choir performed oratorios she would also ask me to sing soprano or alto solos. This experience was to become an important part of my career as a primary teacher specialising in music.

There were two memorial services held for Margaret after she died in her early seventies. All the music students from my year at Malvern Hall were present at the first of these, held at Solihull Methodist church where she had been organist and choir-mistress for almost 50 years, and also the second at Solihull Boys School Chapel, where there was standing-room only. I think the music performed at both did her justice. Such a legacy as the one she has left to the field of music could only be surpassed, in my opinion, by some of the great composers themselves.

On going to Teacher Training College, I upset my French teacher considerably by announcing that I was going to make music my specialist subject rather than French. French had been my great strength during my time at the school, having received several prizes at Birmingham University for the Alliance Française's French-speaking poetry and prose competitions for schools in the area. But music was now well and truly "in my blood" and I wanted desperately to share it with the children I would teach. The fondness for French-speaking is nevertheless still there and has come in very useful since my son bought a holiday villa in the south of the country. My husband also became a regular francophile and we tended to spend many of our vacations travelling in France when our children were small.

My mother's family set great store by the way people speak. Although it was fairly obvious that they were Birmingham folk, the girls in the family did their best to try and lose their local accents, presumably in order to appear slightly higher up the social ladder than their address dictated. The only one to succeed completely was Anne, whose well-modulated vowel sounds belied her humble origins. Our mother had a special and quite convincing voice she used for visitors and speaking in public, whereas Aunt Winnie's flawless French was, to those of us who knew her, quite noticeably accompanied by the characteristic sing-song whine! I don't think it was such a big issue for Aunt Flo, who didn't appear to consider it a problem. The brothers also were perfectly content to remain recognisable Brummies.

So when I brought home my intended, obviously a Birmingham lad, his reception by some of the women in the family was not exactly welcoming.

"You're not going to let her marry *him*, are you, our Marion?" Was Aunt Anne's remark, repeated to me later by my mother who was of the same opinion, purely on account of his accent, regardless of his impressive academic credentials and officer status from his National Service in the RAF.

Unfortunately Victor and my mother were destined never to see eye to eye on anything and quite obviously grew to hate each other. There was a distinct similarity between their personalities in many ways, but I suspect they were both victims of the then little-known-about condition of clinical depression.

It is only since her death that I have considered this a possibility as far as my mother is concerned. It might explain her frequent unaccountable outbursts of temper and verbal aggression, which were levelled mainly at our poor mild-tempered Dad, whose manner of coping when it happened was to take refuge in the garden with his flowers! In my teenage years whenever I was the target of Mum's anger I tended to retaliate and our quarrels were frequently noisy and quite harrowing. My sister managed to avoid scenes like this, though I was surprised quite recently to hear her say that she was often very frightened by Mum's fits of temper.

My husband, on the other hand, had sought medical advice for his depression during his student days. He was referred for psychiatric treatment over a period of about three years and even recommended for neuro-surgery! He did not go ahead with this (these were the notorious fifties when courses of electric shocks and brain surgery were thought to be the answer to everything!) and he eventually decided he did not require further treatment of any kind. Unfortunately his depressive moods affected our life together. Nevertheless, I understood this kind of thing came with the territory of being married to a musician and was willing to accept it. My own temperament did not always cope too well with the quarrels, however, but being very different in character from Victor, it was always easier for me to recover from these episodes than it was for him.

But the music in my life blossomed into something I had never imagined possible. Our initially similar tastes became gradually identical over the years. Our social lives were completely taken up with going to concerts and listening to CDs, particularly when Victor became the classical music correspondent for the local Coventry newspaper that entitled us to free seats and CD recordings!

Victor's violin-playing, in the early days of our acquaintance, was outstanding. After being awarded an exhibition at Birmingham following his university degree, he spent a year at the Paris Conservatoire studying viola.

A few years after we were married he progressed from teaching music in schools to lecturing in Teacher Training, his last post being at Warwick University in Coventry. He also managed to earn extra cash playing in orchestras, especially at Christmas, which was always welcome! Unfortunately he didn't keep this up as the children grew older, saying that his standard of playing had lapsed (in other words he was then unable to keep up the necessary six and seven hours a day practice sessions while earning a living as a university music lecturer!). I don't think this helped his mental state of mind. In my opinion this was a crucial part of what he was, particularly as it had been his vain ambition to be a professional soloist! I regretted not hearing him play the violin and was sorry the children did not witness his daily practice sessions that had previously been the background to our life together. Nevertheless, it did not deter all three of our offspring taking up the subject of music and ultimately using it as a quintessential ingredient in their careers!

In view of these frequent problematic incidents, it was a blessing in some ways that I was able to teach for much of the time when our children were small. I never found the job an easy one and was constantly exhausted, but I was always completely absorbed in what I did in school and enjoyed my professional life up to early retirement at the age of fifty-five, having been in the job for nearly thirty years. I was always aware that my life was a lot happier than it had been before I married. I loved my husband, my job, my home (we made a total of seven moves during our time together!), and, from the age of twenty-nine onwards, being a mum.

Victor's sudden death at sixty-six changed everything. It was not just my husband I missed but the whole world of music he had brought into my life. Our social scene with its busy orbit of concert-going and music involvement died with him. Until that time rarely had there been a week without attendance at a top-quality concert, from Birmingham Symphony Hall to Warwick University Arts Centre as well as Stratford-on-Avon and churches in the surrounding areas, especially in the years he was a newspaper critic.

Apart from singing in choirs, the music in my life following Victor's death tended to be limited to listening to his vast collection of CDs (acquired mainly from the time he reviewed them for the newspaper) as well as to the music programmes on Radio 3. Fortunately both my daughters are also musical and the elder one, Helen, who lives in London, takes me to the occasional concert when I visit her and Rachel, the younger, attends choir rehearsals with me since I came to live near her in Nottingham.

My music teaching has continued to the present day, due to the fact that there is now a dearth of music specialists in primary schools as a result of the National Curriculum and the fact that it is neither a subject of SATS tests nor listed in league tables! I have been a teacher of recorder groups and sometime piano accompanist for the last sixteen years of my official "retirement", even into my early seventies! I regard it as a privilege to be involved with young children and to witness their musical development. It presents me with a motive in life for my older age, (together with being a grandmother to four little ones!).

The Garrison family involvement in music appears to be inescapable. Daughter Helen is a senior producer of music programmes on Radio 3, Rachel a creative arts specialist at the primary school where she teaches and John, the family music rebel, a professional (and successful!) singer-songwriter and session player in the pop world! Long may Garrison music continue!

> Music, when soft voices die,
> Vibrates in the memory —
> Odours, when sweet violets sicken,
> Live within the sense they quicken.
> Rose leaves, when the rose is dead,
> Are heap'd for the beloved's bed;
> And so thy thoughts, when thou are gone,
> Love itself shall slumber on.

Shelley.